☆
☆
☆
☆
☆

LIVING LANGUAGE

☆

USA CULTURE CAPSULES FOR ESL STUDENTS

☆
☆

Jerrilou Johnson
University of the Americas
Mexico

Dialogs on Life in the United States for Students of English as a Second Language

☆
☆
☆
☆
☆

Newbury House Publishers, Inc.
Rowley / Massachusetts / 01969

Library of Congress Cataloging in Publication Data

Johnson, Jerrilou, 1944-
Living language.

1. English language--Text-books for foreigners.
2. Americanisms. I. Title.
PE1128.J6 428'.2'4 78-23495
ISBN 0-88377-152-7

NEWBURY HOUSE PUBLISHERS, INC.

Language Science
Language Teaching
Language Learning

ROWLEY, MASSACHUSETTS 01969

Cover design by KATHE HARVEY.
Artwork by LOIS LEVIT BASILIO.

First printing: February 1979
5 4 3 2

Printed in the U.S.A.

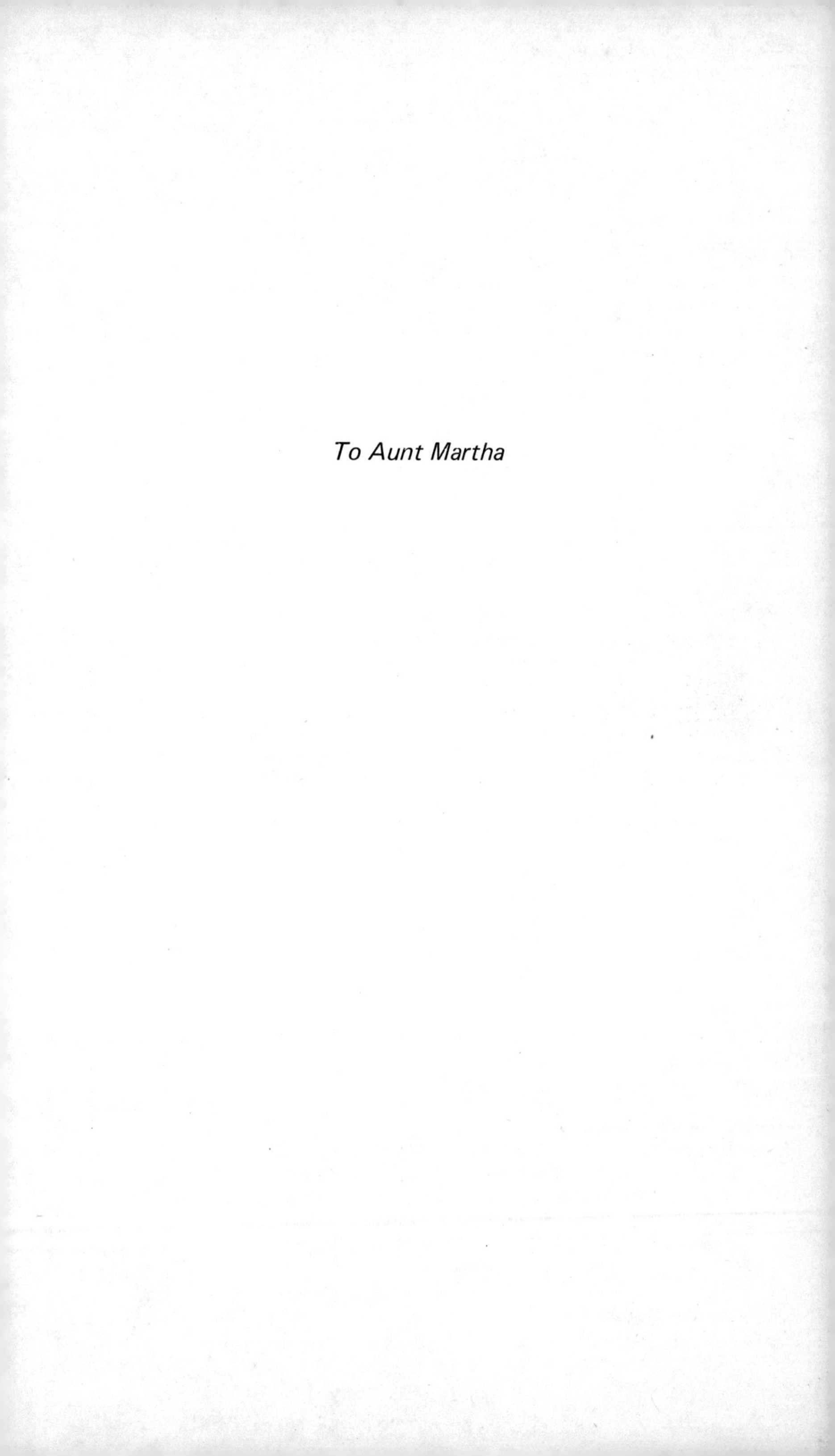

To Aunt Martha

Contents

To the Student

How many times have you heard about the person who studied a foreign language for a year or more in anticipation of living, studying, or working in a foreign country? The student was able to master the pattern drills in class and could even carry on a limited conversation with fellow classmates. But when he stepped off the airplane, suddenly he felt as if he had no understanding of the language. Nothing sounded right. The patterns weren't the same. He tried to communicate with people, and they reacted as if they didn't understand a word he said. So in quiet desperation, the new arrival anxiously looked for someone who spoke his mother language, someone who could help him out. Sound familiar? Maybe you've even experienced that same frustration. Or perhaps you have heard of people who lived through this experience and you want to avoid it. Either way, this book was written for you. It is an attempt to offer you an opportunity to practice your English, refine your oral and/or written ability, and at the same time learn something about the culture of the United States.

Speaking a second language is difficult enough; but when you try to use it inside a new culture where life styles and basic values are totally different from those with which you have grown up, there are often many problems. Many of these problems are unnecessary, and the frustrations you experience trying to resolve them use an enormous amount of energy which could be directed to more productive goals. An awareness of some basic life styles in the United States can enable students learning English to feel more comfortable as they try to function in a new culture. After you finish these ten culture capsules, you should have some understanding of the following aspects of U.S. culture:

- Unemployment
- Singles' life
- Shopping
- Education
- Urban development
- Divorce

- Family unity
- Racism
- The position of women

The purpose of these capsules is not to teach you one specific way of thinking about any particular aspect of United States culture. Rather, they are designed to help you analyze different areas of culture in the United States and compare them with your native culture, so that you will develop a broader understanding of life in the United States and a greater fluency in the English language.

The desired result is that when you find yourself in situations which pose both language and cultural problems, your ability to communicate will not be limited by your lack of cultural understanding of life in the United States. The capsules do not attempt to make any value judgments with regard to United States culture. You may make these judgments for yourself after some investigations and thinking of your own. Finally, you should feel more confidence in your ability to understand life in the United States, to make your own decisions regarding controversial issues, and to express yourself better in English.

An Introduction for Instructors

One of the biggest needs I found during my years of experience teaching English as a second language (ESL) was for a book which included information about the culture of the United States. Most students who study English in their native countries do so in anticipation of traveling, working, studying, even living in the United States. Linguistic preparation is not sufficient to prepare students for the many cultural differences they will encounter upon arrival in the United States. Not only are holidays, working hours, eating schedules, and classroom procedures often very different from those of the students' native cultures, but also basic ideas and attitudes toward life are totally different from those of their mother cultures. When students must cope with linguistic expression and comprehension, in addition to attitudinal and value changes, they often find themselves unable to function at their optimum in either area.

BACKGROUND

This book was developed as an attempt to fill this void along with a review of English at the intermediate to advanced level within the context of United States culture. The work began as part of my graduate work at the University of the Americas in Mexico City, Mexico. That particular geographical setting provided an excellent opportunity to use the various capsules with Mexican students studying English in Mexico City. The capsules have been used in a variety of teaching situations, but the most extensive use was at CENLEMEX, Centro de Lenguas de la Cuidad de Mexico, where junior adult and adult students study English as a second language from beginning to advanced levels. The capsules were used at a high intermediate level as supplementary materials. They have also been used in private teaching situations where business executives want to "brush up" on their use of English in anticipation of an extensive trip to the United States. In these instances the capsules were the sole text for a thirty-hour course. Working on a one-to-one basis, students do not need the expected four hours to complete each capsule.

Teachers have responded favorably to use of the culture capsules, feeling that they give a certain amount of necessary structure to the class but at the same time provide sufficient flexibility for teachers to adapt each capsule to individual classes, emphasizing written or oral skills as dictated by specific needs.

Students reacted positively to the materials, emphasizing their desire to work within the framework of United States culture as they concentrated on those areas of ESL in which they felt deficient. Subject matter seemed varied enough and offered a sufficient variety of perspectives to enable students ranging in age from young adolescents to adult executives to find a point of identification in their mother culture which could be transferred to the new culture. It seemed to be a positive factor that students were able to talk about and discuss their native culture in their second language, English, and then compare the culture which they know with the culture they want to learn about. Even in Mexico City, where all the students were Mexicans, there were cultural differences in the same classroom when students came from outlying provincial areas as opposed to large urban areas. This would be even more pronounced in a class where the student body comes from a variety of different backgrounds. With that thought in mind, teachers should be sure to allow sufficient time in class to permit students to discuss their own native cultures at length before comparing them with the United States culture.

OUTSIDE THE UNITED STATES

Living Language can be used outside the United States for English language teaching at an intermediate-advanced level for students who want or need to have a broader understanding of United States culture. In this sense the material will help to prepare students for many of the cultural differences they will encounter in the United States. It is hoped that the study of these culture capsules will make the student's entrance into the target culture an easier, more positive, less painful experience. The wide variety of exercises in each of the capsules gives students a chance to develop intermediate listening comprehension, speaking, reading, and writing skills in a cross-cultural situation. Although each capsule focuses on a few aspects of United States culture, there is always, within the capsule, an opportunity for students to refer to their native cultures.

INSIDE THE UNITED STATES

For students who are already living in the United States and have an intermediate level of language proficiency but who still need to "polish up" their English, this material provides such an opportunity. Listening comprehension, as well as written and spoken expression, are all emphasized within a cross-cultural context. In each capsule students will analyze their new life style in relation to their native cultures. This offers students material which they know and understand as a basis to explore cross-cultural communication situations.

Students who finish these culture capsules:

- Will have a wider understanding of United States culture
- Will have a more secure feeling about themselves in relation to various social situations in the United States
- Will have a stronger ability to evaluate, for themselves, controversial issues involved with United States culture

CLASSROOM PROCEDURE

There are two ways to begin working with each capsule. The first way is to have students listen to the tape, read aloud the dialog, and answer the Comprehension Questions before they work with the two sections on vocabulary. That is, vocabulary work is an outgrowth of the dialog. The second way is to work with Vocabulary Review Sections B and C first, to prepare students for the dialog they will hear later. In some capsules, one method is preferable for various reasons. When that is the case, it is clearly stated in the Instructor's Notes. For the most part, however, that decision depends entirely on the instructors, and how comfortable they feel working with the materials, and which method they feel is best suited to their classrooms. In any case, the procedure should be varied to eliminate monotony of classroom routine. However, regardless of which method the teacher uses, students should never be asked to read the dialog aloud or take part in role-playing of the dialog until they have heard it on tape or read by the teacher. That is, students should not be expected to produce sounds until they have first been exposed to the model expression and intonation. Lifeless mechanical reading should be avoided.

Before attempting to have students assume roles for oral reading of the dialog, the instructor should make sure there are no questions regarding vocabulary. The Vocabulary section lists specific words related to the theme of each capsule, as well as verbs, everyday phrases, and where it is used, slang. The words marked by an asterisk (*) denote key words or phrases which the student should be sure to understand. Some of these words may not be found in any dictionary; so Instructor's Notes for each capsule define these words or phrases which should receive special attention. It is important that the students understand these words in the context of the dialog and also in a more general context. For this reason the Vocabulary Review section affords the opportunity to put these words into new contexts.

Once the teacher is certain that there are no problems related to the new vocabulary or to the dialogs in general, students are ready to read the dialog, role-playing wherever possible. If, for example, there is an all-male class and an all-female dialog, the teacher may elect to omit that capsule or to approach it from a more objective third person perspective rather than from the identification of the first person, unless students themselves insist and volunteer to play the female roles.

The Comprehension Questions section gives both teacher and student an excellent opportunity to evaluate students' comprehension of the situation in the dialog, as well as comprehension of the vocabulary that has been used. Not much class time should be spent on this section. Questions should be answered orally. Later, for additional work with written skills, the teacher may want to have students write out answers to the questions. However, the purpose of these questions is not to motivate class discussion but to ensure that the students understand the essential ideas presented in the dialog.

Having completed the Vocabulary sections and Comprehension Questions, the class is ready to move on to the core of the culture capsule. The majority of time and teaching effort should be directed to Questions for Discussion and Suggested Activities.

While working with the Questions for Discussion, instructors will have to draw on their own personal resources. This should present no problem to a teacher who is a native to United States culture. To nonnative teachers the Instructor's Notes for each capsule should be helpful. Teachers should be reminded that the purpose of the culture capsule is to encourage free exchange of ideas on sometimes controversial issues, as well as to inform the student about the target culture. With this in mind, instructors should try to keep their own contribution to a minimum, at all times encouraging an active intellectual exchange among the students. To give more life to the lesson and make it more meaningful, the instructor may ask students to compare the specific topic being discussed with their own cultures.

The Suggested Activities give students various possibilities for their own self-expression. It is not intended that all the activities which are listed be completed by each student. The wide range of activities, from written to oral expression, offers something to attract the personality and needs of each one. Several of the suggested activities would lend themselves nicely to the idea of a term project. That is, if students demonstrate a particular interest in one of the topics related to a specific capsule, they may want to do some deeper investigation or research into that particular area. These possible term projects are mentioned in the Instructor's Notes of each capsule. Working with such a term project would provide an excellent opportunity for instruction on use of the library, the use of the *Readers' Guide to Periodical Literature,* and a more formal approach to written expression. Obviously, this type of project would not be suited to all classes and should be included only when the instructor sees that the needs of the class or of individual students determine such projects.

Instructor's Notes

CAPSULE ONE

In order that students may enjoy and understand the more subtle humor of the dialog, the teacher may want to prepare them before they read the dialog or listen to the tape, by working with the Vocabulary and Vocabulary Review sections. Have students look over the list of words and ask questions about any unfamiliar word. If possible, have other students answer the questions of fellow students. It is not expected that students will be able to spell and define each word, but they should be able to recognize each word in context. Vocabulary Review may be used as homework or may be done in class. For homework, students may like to try to write original sentences using some of the vocabulary words.

It is important that the words with more than one meaning are clearly understood. Although students may be familiar with one definition, another may be completely foreign to them. For example: *limousine* as an expensive chauffeur-driven private car and as an inexpensive means of travel from the airport to the center of a city; *fine* as an adjective and as a noun, meaning a sum to be paid for an infraction of the law; *stories* as reading matter and as the number of floors of a building; *plants* as growing matter and as another word for factories. Perhaps visuals depicting the two different meanings of each word would be the best way of presenting these differences.

Questions for Discussion

1. If students themselves do not bring up this idea, the teacher should interject the thought of the changing image of cab drivers, i.e., college graduates, housewives, etc. This is a good opportunity at the beginning of the course to introduce the concept of a stereotype. The cab driver in the dialog is a stereotype. But stereotyped images limit our understanding of a culture. Ask students to give examples of other stereotypes—for example, the Mexican under his sombrero, leaning against a cactus, with his burro standing patiently nearby.

2. This question offers a good opportunity to discuss the "melting pot" theory of United States society. Since most students will not have come from a country with the same mixture of races, it is unlikely that they will have so many different neighborhoods.
3. Since David asked the cab driver why his wife didn't pay off the policeman, it is possible that he might have tried to resolve the problem in this way. Encourage students to be candid about discussing this procedure as operating in their own countries. Don't try to conceal these types of operations in the United States. Rather, open up the discussion to include Watergate, Lockheed, and other situations of this kind.

Suggested Activities

It is not essential that the class participate in all the suggested activities. The wide variety of activities allows the teacher and student to select those which best suit the level and the personality of the student. For example, with the first activity the teacher may, with better classes or students, encourage students to develop this list into a composition.

Activity 5 may be done as a term project rather than a short activity for one lesson. This would permit the student more time to get into the subject in depth. Term projects could be presented throughout the semester, or at the end.

CAPSULE TWO

The teacher may want to prepare students to read or hear the dialog by first working with the Vocabulary and Vocabulary Review sections. Or the teacher may prefer to leave the vocabulary work as an outgrowth of students' having heard or read the dialog. Either method is acceptable, and this should be determined by the class level and needs. Before going on to work with the Questions for Discussion and Suggested Activities, be sure students understand the Comprehension Questions. When working with the Vocabulary Review section the teacher may want to ask students to write more original sentences using the words from the Vocabulary section. Be sure that the vocabulary words marked by an asterisk (*) are understood by the students.

The teacher should check to be sure that students make the distinction in pronunciation between *divorce* and *divorcee.*

The author Anaïs Nin is mentioned in the last part of the dialog. Ask students if they have heard of her writings and encourage stronger students, with an interest in the area of feminist thinking, to read the *Diaries of Anaïs Nin.*

Questions for Discussion

Encourage students to be as open as possible about their own feelings and their cultural conditioning with regard to divorce. Be sure to discuss not only the divorced woman but also the divorced man. Try to bring out any differences in attitudes toward the divorced woman and the divorced man. When students have strong pro or con feelings regarding divorce, try to have them explore the cultural conditioning which may have formed these strong feelings. They may come, for example, from a Roman Catholic country or from a country where divorce does not exist.

CAPSULE THREE

Once again, be sure that vocabulary words marked with an asterisk (*) are understood by the students before continuing with the rest of the lesson. To clarify for the students the idea of a conservative dresser (as used in the dialog), it might be easiest to use visuals, cut out from magazines, which portray the extremes of dress code. The blue suit, white shirt, tie; the "mod" look; the formal look; the casual look: all lend themselves nicely to work with visuals. Students can discuss where one look is more appropriate than another.

As an outgrowth of the dialog encourage students to discuss how Father's Day and Mother's Day are celebrated in their native countries. Which of the two days, if either, is given preference? Are they celebrated on the same day each year?

Questions for Discussion

Students are sure to have varying opinions regarding the first question. Encourage a lively and candid discussion among students of differing opinions. Ask students if this particular gift-giving procedure exists in their native countries. Question 2 should provide an interesting exchange of cross-cultural values, as students will answer this question depending on their own perspectives. Making these kinds of value judgments in a second culture and in a second language is not easy. If students are able to make these judgments for the characters in the dialog, they should have a better chance of being able to transfer this type of knowledge to their own real-life situations.

Suggested Activities

The teacher should select activities which are most appropriate to the individual level of the class. Individual students with a need to improve oral skills should be encouraged to participate in Activities 3 and 4. Activity 6 should be done by students with an interest in developing writing skills. Activities 1 and 2 may be done in oral or written form.

CAPSULE FOUR

The vocabulary in this capsule is not particularly difficult and is very much related to the daily lives of students; therefore, it might be interesting first to let students hear the dialog on tape and read the dialog, rather than prepare them for the dialog with previous vocabulary work. When working with Section C of the Vocabulary Review, the teacher should put the following list of words on the blackboard while students are reading the short paragraph. These words will serve as a guide for the exercise and, if desired, for a class discussion regarding the information given in the short paragraph.

> produce, reasonably priced, pleasant surprise, come upon, farm-fresh, settling for, supermarket, take advantage of

Perhaps visuals would be the clearest way to differentiate between *produce,* the verb, and the noun which is used in this lesson, meaning that which is grown by farming. Be sure that the pronunciation for each meaning is clearly understood.

Questions for Discussion

In addition to answering the given questions, be sure to encourage students to share with the class the eating habits that are typical of their native countries. Encourage a cross-cultural exchange of these customs. For example, ask students what is the typical snack in their countries, e.g., the taco in Mexico.

Suggested Activities

Activity 1 is another possibility of a term project for some students who demonstrate a special interest in this topic.

For activity 4 ask students to bring in an ad from a United States magazine for a garbage disposal or for "junk food."

If the class situation lends itself, this would be a good opportunity to have an international buffet. Students could bring dishes that are typical of their native countries.

CAPSULE FIVE

The vocabulary level of this lesson is such that students might feel more secure listening to the tape and reading the dialog if they have first worked with the Vocabulary and Vocabulary Review sections. In the Vocabulary Review section encourage the students to read aloud to the class the original sentences they have written.

Questions for Discussion

The whole issue of couples "living together" should provide a wealth of interesting material for discussion. Be sure to encourage the students to be open and honest with their feelings. Ask questions like, "What effect does this kind of situation have on family unity or family stability?" Question 6 could be developed to where students list jobs which they feel go into the three categories. This should promote all kinds of class discussion. Be sure with question 8 to spend sufficient time to establish what percentage of tip is expected in restaurants. It is not enough that students think in terms of a flat 10 or 15 percent tip. If a cup of coffee is 40 cents, a 10 percent tip would be 4 cents and a 15 percent tip would be 6 cents. Neither would be appropriate. The teacher may want to list ten different amounts on the blackboard and have students comment on the appropriate tip for each amount.

Suggested Activities

The first activity is another possibility for a term project for a student who exhibits a special interest in this particular area of discussion. If students like the idea of working with the mini-drama, include variations of the suggested situation. For example, she tries to pay (it's his birthday) and he won't let her; he starts to pay and realizes that he left his wallet at home; he doesn't have enough money to pay the bill; the bill comes and she suggests that they split it (they're just office friends and happened to sit together at the coffee break).

CAPSULE SIX

Because of the large vocabulary in this capsule the teacher may want to work with the Vocabulary section and the Vocabulary Review section before listening to the dialog on tape and reading it. Although in all probability this will not offer any specific problem to students, it may be a good time to present *thorough* (meaning *complete*) as opposed to *through, threw, (al)though, thought; weight, weigh, way;* and the other groups of words that are listed in Section B of the Vocabulary Review section.

Questions for Discussion

When discussing the first question, be sure to introduce the whole concept of summer jobs and part-time jobs for students. Although this is very common in the United States, it is not so common in other countries, especially in Latin America. Students whose parents can afford to send them to university rarely work. The concept of a student who doesn't need to work and yet has a summer job may be entirely new to your students. Shirley may not have to work. She never says directly that her parents pay her university expenses, but she has time and money to indulge in skiing and tennis. It might be argued, however, that she works in the summer in order to afford herself the luxury of these things when she is at school.

Many countries outside the United States do not have strict regulation of amphetamines. When discussing question 5, be sure to emphasize the illegality of the misuse of these pills, as well as the harmful effects on one's health.

Suggested Activities

It is possible that there may be a doctor or nurse in the class. If this is the case, be sure to use him/her as a resource person in this capsule.

When students are discussing activity 3, do not neglect to introduce the idea of "junk food" as a medical problem. The United States is not the only country where this problem exists.

CAPSULE SEVEN

It is probably best to begin working with this capsule by studying the Vocabulary and Vocabulary Review sections before listening to the tape or reading the dialog. Be sure that students know the asterisked words, as well as the other words listed in the Vocabulary section.

When working with Section C of the Vocabulary Review, the teacher should put the following list of words on the blackboard while students are reading the short paragraph. These words should serve as a guide for a class discussion regarding the information given in the paragraph:

> prefer, built better, less expensive, resistence, someone else's problems, mechanically inclined, garage, minor repairs, mechanic

Questions for Discussion

When establishing Genie and Bob's socioeconomic level, be sure the class included Genie's education, the fact that the couple buys on installment, Genie's southern background, and Bob's (implied) northern background. In question 3 be sure that the class is aware of the facility presented by installment buying but that the high monthly interest rates are not always in the best interest of the buyer. When discussing racial prejudice encourage students to share experiences they may have had, as opposed to making third party judgments on any given country. When the subject of racial prejudice in the United States is introduced, the teacher should try to elicit a possible explanation (e.g., the "melting-pot" theory), for the existence of this prejudice.

The phrase used by Bob is well known to black people. There were many references to this phrase in black literature of the 1920s. It may be considered a forerunner of the phrase "black is beautiful," made popular in the 1960s, as it is praising the beauty of darker people, to counteract the prejudice in favor of lighter-skinned people. Using the symbolism of a darker berry which is juicier than a not-yet-ripe (thus not as dark) berry, the saying implies the sweetness of dark-skinned people.

Suggested Activities

All the activities in this section are not meant to be performed or accomplished by all the students. Students may wish to choose between activity 2 and activity 5 as a narrative composition. Since activity 4 is the first persuasive type of writing students have been asked to do, this should not be eliminated; but if they prefer to make an oral persuasive presentation, this should be acceptable. If a student prefers not to discuss the experience of activity 5 with the class, he should be permitted to write a composition rather than make an oral presentation.

When working with the mini-drama, try to inject humor into the classroom. Don't allow the women to fall into the stereotyped woman car buyer, as portrayed by Genie. Encourage the women in class to prepare activity 1 and then take part in the mini-drama. With their newly acquired information the women should be able to prepare a lively discussion with the car salesman.

CAPSULE EIGHT

Because of the use of rather unusual speech patterns in the dialog, it is probably best to prepare the students with vocabulary work before they listen to the tape or attempt to read the dialog. Wherever possible, try to have students from the class answer other students' questions about the vocabulary. The teacher should be sure to explain the concept of compensation (unemployment compensation) as used in the dialog, in addition to the general meaning of the word. To be sure that students remember *plant,* used as *factory* (in the first capsule), the teacher may want to use the same visuals for a fast classroom review. Also, visuals may be used to show the difference between *checkers,* the game; a *check-out* clerk; and *checked* fabric. If possible, a picture of a *truck stop* and a picture of a "regular" restaurant would be a good way to present the differences in the food, service, hours of service, etc., in the different types of restaurants. In working with such an extensive vocabulary list the teacher might want to assign one of the phrases or verb phrases to students as homework, asking that they find the meanings and report to the next class. Answers to C of the Vocabulary Review should be put on the board and discussed.

Questions for Discussion

Be sure that the class includes lack of education, limited experience, lack of training, and age as factors contributing to Willard's difficulty in finding a job. Visuals may be an excellent way to present the idea of blue-collar and white-collar workers. If the teacher brings to class ten or twelve different pictures from magazines, the class can try to put the pictures into the proper category. Be sure that students understand clearly the distinction between the two definitions. Question 6 can lead to a discussion of dialects, standard vs. nonstandard speech, appropriateness of language, etc.

Suggested Activities

Before students are asked actually to participate in the mini-drama as suggested, the class as a whole might discuss various attitudes, fears, and insecurities that could be part of the discussion between the two women.

If you are teaching outside the United States, you can ask students who have friends in the United States to write to them asking for information regarding questions 3 and 4.

CAPSULE NINE

As in the preceding capsule the teacher should be the one to decide whether students work first with the dialog or with the Vocabulary sections.

Labor Day, the workingman's holiday, is celebrated the first Monday in September. Unlike other holidays it has neither political nor religious origin, nor is it celebrated in any uniform way. It comes at the end of summer so that almost everyone, employer as well as employee, in business, industry, government, agriculture, even the self-employed, closes up shop and enjoys the long weekend before school reopens and fall business activities begin. However, some large stores hold sales on this day.

Be sure that students understand the different names for parts of a house and pieces of furniture. The instructor may want to prepare visuals from decorating magazines, as a means of testing or reviewing. Explain the difference between parquet floors and regular wooden floors.

Questions for Discussion

When discussing question 3 be sure that beer is recognized as a short-term goal of both men. Bill's long-term goal is to be a doctor. Steve's short-term goal is to pay off the debts he has. His longer-term goal is a trip to South America. Neither man seems to see "settling down" as either a short- or long-term goal. In question 4 mention other situations which might produce problems, such as a mixed couple, homosexuals, or an extremely old single person. In the discussion of question 5 don't overlook the possibility of a double standard in this situation. Whereas it might be acceptable for two young men to move away from home, it might not be acceptable for two young women. Introduce here the question of a society's imposed values.

Suggested Activities

In activity 2 the teacher may want to interject other problem situations, such as those mentioned above. Activity 6 is an excellent way to help students extend and review vocabulary. Activity 4 is practical and should not be overlooked. If a student in the class is apartment hunting, ask students to bring in an ad which sounds as if it may meet the student's needs. This activity also provides an excellent opportunity to discuss the different neighborhood sections in a particular city or town. This is an important element in apartment hunting.

CAPSULE TEN

It should be the teacher's decision whether students first listen to the tape and read the dialog, followed by the Comprehension Questions, or whether students first work with the Vocabulary and Vocabulary Review sections as preparation for hearing the dialog.

Questions for Discussion

1. The fact that the Scotts have a big yard, a grill, a doghouse, storm windows, patio furniture, friends with a summer cottage, and a daughter who plays tennis indicates rather clearly that they are basically a middle-class family. The fact that lunch is bought at the local McDonald's may (or may not) place them more low to middle, middle class.
2. The fenced yard, the planned tennis game, the ability to "run over" to McDonald's all indicate that this scene took place in a town, probably suburban.
3. The availability of household servants in many countries removes the do-it-yourself need.

Suggested Activities

For many students, the Day of the Dead, or Halloween, will be the day celebrated in memory of lost loved ones. Be sure that students are aware of the United States Halloween as something different. You might suggest as an addition activity that one of the students research the origin of the United States Halloween.

LIVING LANGUAGE

☆

USA CULTURE CAPSULES FOR ESL STUDENTS

CAPSULE ONE

☆☆☆☆☆

City Streets

DIALOG

David: Where can I find a taxi, please?

Airline Agent: Do you want a cab or a limousine?

David: Well, . . . I . . . I want a taxi.

Agent: Walk outside and turn left. You'll find the taxi stop.

David: Thanks.

[He walks outside and finds a cab.]

Driver: Where to?

David: Palmer House Hotel, please.

Driver: Wow! Why didn't you take the limousine? You must be loaded.

David: Loaded? . . . I . . .

Driver: Loaded—you know, rich. Why didn't you take the limo? It goes directly to the Palmer House and only costs three bucks.

David: Oh, I didn't know. I thought the limousine meant a private rented car.

Driver: No way! The limousine is the big airport bus that shuttles from the airport to the city.

David: Shuttle?

Driver: Shuttle! You know—goes back and forth from the airport to the downtown area. Hey! Where are you from?

David: Mexico City.

Driver: You're a long way from home. What are you doing here?

David: I'm going to be studying for a year at the University of Chicago.

Driver: U. of C.? Are you a genius or something? Is that all the luggage you have for one year? Man, you should see what some people bring for one week!

David: My parents are sending the majority of my books and luggage air freight.

Driver: This your first time in Chicago?

David: Yes. Pardon me, but is there always so much traffic here in Chicago?

Driver: Traffic is really heavy now 'cause it's the rush hour.

David: Rush hour? Excuse me, but what is rush hour?

Driver: "Rush hour" means when all the people are rushing to get to work in the morning or rushing to get home in the evening. Many of the people who work in the offices downtown have to come in from the suburbs; so the workers who live in the inner city have to go out to the suburbs every day. It's a crazy world.

David: So a lot of people need this large . . . uh . . . *periferico*.

Driver: Pair of what? Man, this is an expressway; it's a main thoroughfare that cuts across the entire city. We're passing through the old industrial area now. That's downtown ahead. The suburbs are over there to your left. You should have seen all the traffic jams before they built the expressways. See all those big trailer trucks? They have to stay in the two right-hand lanes. Before the expressways were built all those big trucks were going to and from the city every day on the regular streets. It was impossible. Now the city has made special streets into avenues and boulevards; no trucks are allowed on these streets—only cars.

David: And do the people obey the traffic laws?

Driver: Yep! Chicago police enforce the city laws. Why, last week my wife got a ticket for jaywalking downtown. Can you believe that?

David: Jaywalking?

Driver: That's when you cross the street in the middle of the block instead of crossing at the corner with the traffic light.

David: Did she go to jail?

Driver: Well, I felt like sending her to jail but she just paid the fine instead of going to traffic court.

David: Was it not possible for her to pay the policeman some money so he would not give her the ticket?

Driver: No way! Payoff is a tricky business here. The mayor's office is cracking down. You see that tall black building with the rabbit ears on top?

David: Yes.

Driver: That's the John Hancock Building—used to be the tallest building in the world until Sears Roebuck built that big building you see straight ahead. Now it's the tallest in the world. But I heard some city in Europe is trying to build one even higher. Well, that's progress.

David: What are the buildings used for?

Driver: John Hancock has very fancy department stores on the ground floor, and a bank, I think. In front of it is an ice skating rink, sort of like Rockefeller Center in New York, they say. The upper stories are real ritzy apartments. Sears? I don't know. I guess all their big central offices are in that building. Can you believe it—132 stories of Sears Roebuck? Hey, what hotel did you say?

David: Palmer House, please.

Driver: Oh, yeah. That's first class living, huh?

David: It's the only hotel I know in Chicago. A friend gave me the name of it.

Driver: Some friend! Must be rich this friend. Not many students can afford the Palmer House.

David: It's just for tonight. Tomorrow I'll go to the University of Chicago.

Driver: U. of C. South side. Real rough neighborhood, some people say.

David: I have heard that the neighborhood is very cosmopolitan; there are students from all over the world living near the university.

Driver: Yes. That neighborhood is called Hyde Park. Used to be a real good, solid, middle-class neighborhood. But it's changing, real fast, or so people say. I live on the southwest side of the city. Old neighborhood. First generation Italian. This area we're passing through now is an old Greek neighborhood. Great restaurants—cheap too, if you know where to go. But the city is tearing down lots of this area. Urban renewal. They say they are going to build new high-rise apartments. We're on the edge of downtown now. There's more traffic than usual 'cause the stores are open late tonight.

David: The stores are open late on Thursday nights?

Driver: Yep! Usually they close at 5:30 but on Monday and Thursday nights they are open to 7:30 or 8:00. My ol' lady likes to come downtown on the subway on Thursday, catch the 2 o'clock movie before the prices go up, and then go shopping until the stores close. That's how she got her ticket last Thursday, jaywalking in front of the subway station.

David: Does the subway go to the University of Chicago?

Driver: Nope! You'll have to take the train at the Randolph Street Station. It's only four blocks from your hotel. Well, here we are. That'll be $14.30, tip not included.

David: $14.30!!!!!?????

Driver: Man, that's why I said you should have taken the limo. It only costs three dollars and it comes right to this hotel. Maybe that's why your friend told you to come to this hotel.

David: Maybe. Here's fifteen dollars. Keep the change.

Driver: Look, man, it's okay this time . . . you're just a student, and a stranger here and everything. But just so you know in the future–seventy cents ain't no tip on a $14.30 fare.

COMPREHENSION QUESTIONS

1. Why didn't David take the limousine to the hotel?
2. How long will David be staying in Chicago? Why?
3. Why aren't trailer trucks allowed on avenues and boulevards?
4. According to the story, what is the tallest building in the world?
5. How long will David stay at the Palmer House? Why is he staying there?
6. Judging from the dialog, at what time of day do you think this situation took place?
7. How much luggage did David have when he arrived at the airport? Why?
8. Where does the cab driver live? Describe his neighborhood.
9. Describe one aspect of urban renewal in Chicago.
10. What was the problem with the amount of tip that David gave the driver? Explain.

VOCABULARY

Words Used in Dialog

block
cab
corner
cosmopolitan
downtown
expressway
fare
fine
jaywalking
limousine (limo)
mayor
plants
scholarship
stories
suburb (suburban)
subway
thoroughfare
traffic
traffic light

Phrases

Can you believe that?
clustered around
comes right to (the hotel)*
good solid neighborhood*
got a ticket*
ground floor
heavy traffic
high-rise apartments
ice skating rink
right-hand lane
rush hour
straight ahead
tearing down
tip not included
traffic court
traffic jam
urban renewal*

Verbs

afford
assume
catch (a movie)*
commute
enforce
jaywalk
rush
shuttle

Slang

ain't
cracking down*
hey!
loaded*
man
my ol' lady*
no way
touchy business
wow!
yeah
yep*

*Words listed in the glossary at the end of each capsule.

VOCABULARY REVIEW

afford
assume
catch
clustered around
commute
cracking down
downtown
enforce
fare
get a ticket
ground floor
jaywalking
loaded
neighborhood
rush
rush hour
subway
tear down
thoroughfare
touchy
traffic court
traffic jam
urban renewal

A. Fill in the blanks with words or phrases listed in the Vocabulary Review above.

1. Bribing a policeman can get you into trouble.
   Bribing a policeman is a ______ business.

2. Many people prefer to live in the city rather than have to drive back and forth from the suburbs to the city every day.
   Many people prefer to live in the city rather than have to ______ from the suburbs to the city every day.

3. He gets home late every day because of the heavy traffic on the expressway between 4:30 and 6:30.
   He gets home late every day because of the heavy ______ traffic.

4. Crossing the street in the middle of the block is dangerous because drivers aren't prepared for crossing pedestrians.
   ______ is dangerous because drivers aren't prepared for crossing pedestrians.

5. If we have dinner at 6:00 we will still have time to go to the movies at 8:30.
   If we have dinner at 6:00 we can still ______ the 8:30 movie.

6. Many people would like to move to the suburbs, but they don't have sufficient money to pay the high taxes.
   Many people would like to move to the suburbs but they can't ______ the high taxes.

7. Sometimes it's difficult for parents to make children go to bed at a specific time.
   Sometimes it's difficult for parents to ______ a specific bedtime for children.

8. My wife takes it for granted that we will go to the movies on Saturday.
   My children __________ that we will go to the movies on Saturday.

9. The enormous number of slow-moving cars on the expressway was horrible this morning.
   The __________ on the expressway was horrible this morning.

10. From the way John spends his money he must have a lot of it.
    From the way John spends his money he must be __________.

B. Which of the words or phrases listed in the Vocabulary Review above could be used meaningfully in the following sentences?

1. I got a ticket for speeding last week, so I have to go to __________ this Thursday.
2. I almost __________ for not stopping at the stop sign, but the policeman only gave me a warning.
3. The __________ is also called the first floor; in many other countries the first floor is what we call the second floor in the United States.
4. To avoid the trattic jam at rush hour, I think I'll take the __________ downtown.
5. The city is building a new expressway which goes from __________ to the suburbs.

C. Use each group of words and phrases in the given order and form them to make an original and meaningful sentence.

Example: saw a movie / yesterday / downtown
John saw a movie yesterday when he went downtown.

1. got a ticket / last week / traffic court
2. ice skating rink / ground floor / shopping center
3. scholarship / to study / urban development
4. heavy traffic / rush hour / traffic jam / late to work
5. government / tearing down / high-rise apartments

QUESTIONS FOR DISCUSSION

1. Does the cab driver have a college education? How do you know? Give examples to explain your answer.

2. Do the large cities in your native country have neighborhoods like the ones described in the dialog? If yes, give examples. If no, explain why not.

3. If David had been given a ticket for jaywalking, how might he have tried to handle the situation? Why? How would you react to this situation in your native country? Explain. How would you react to this situation in the United States? Explain.

4. Does your native country have a program like urban renewal? If so, what changes has it created in your country? If not, why do you think there isn't such a program? Do you think there should be? Explain. What are some of the positive and negative aspects of urban renewal?

5. What do you think the cab driver meant when he referred to one section of the city as a "changing neighborhood"? What do you think he meant was changing?

6. The cab driver told David that people who work downtown in the offices are moving to the suburbs. And he said that people who are working in the factories which have moved out to the suburbs live in the city. What groups of people are moving to the suburbs to live? How are these changes affecting the population of large cities?

SUGGESTED ACTIVITIES

1. Make a list of words which you feel describe the sights, sounds, smells, and feelings of "rush hour." This can be "rush hour" on the expressway or in the subway or on public transportation.

2. Tell about "rush hour" in the city which you know best. Is it any different from "rush hour" as you know it in the United States? How?

3. What changes have you observed over the past few years in any city with which you are familiar? Has there been a growth of the suburbs? Has the downtown or central area of the city changed?

Write a composition telling about these changes. You might want to divide the composition into three paragraphs: the first to discuss changes in the buildings, the second to discuss changes in the streets and patterns of life, and the third to discuss changes in the kinds of people who live in different areas.

4. With other members of the class, prepare a mini-drama in which a stranger in town prepares to leave a taxi without paying a tip.

5. Collect articles which discuss plans for changing your city (housing, transportation, recreation, etc.). Report your findings in an oral or written project. Include in your discussion arguments for and against the changes.

GLOSSARY

Phrases

catch a movie—the important item to stress here is the phrase "to catch," meaning to go to see, as opposed to "to catch" a bus or plane.

comes right to the hotel—the key part of this phrase is "comes right to." For example, the ocean comes right to the front of the lawn; the bus comes right to the corner; the newspaper comes right to my door.

good solid neighborhood—an area which reflects a certain stability of the people who live there.

got a ticket—be sure the students understand the difference between "to have" a ticket for a plane and "to get" a ticket for an infraction of the law.

urban renewal—a government-funded program which is responsible for many changes in city planning and construction.

Nonstandard English

cracking down—being very strict.

loaded—having a lot of money; also, being drunk.

my ol' lady—a disrespectful or humorous term for a mother or wife; the opposite of *vieja*—an affectionate expression in Spanish.

yep—yes.

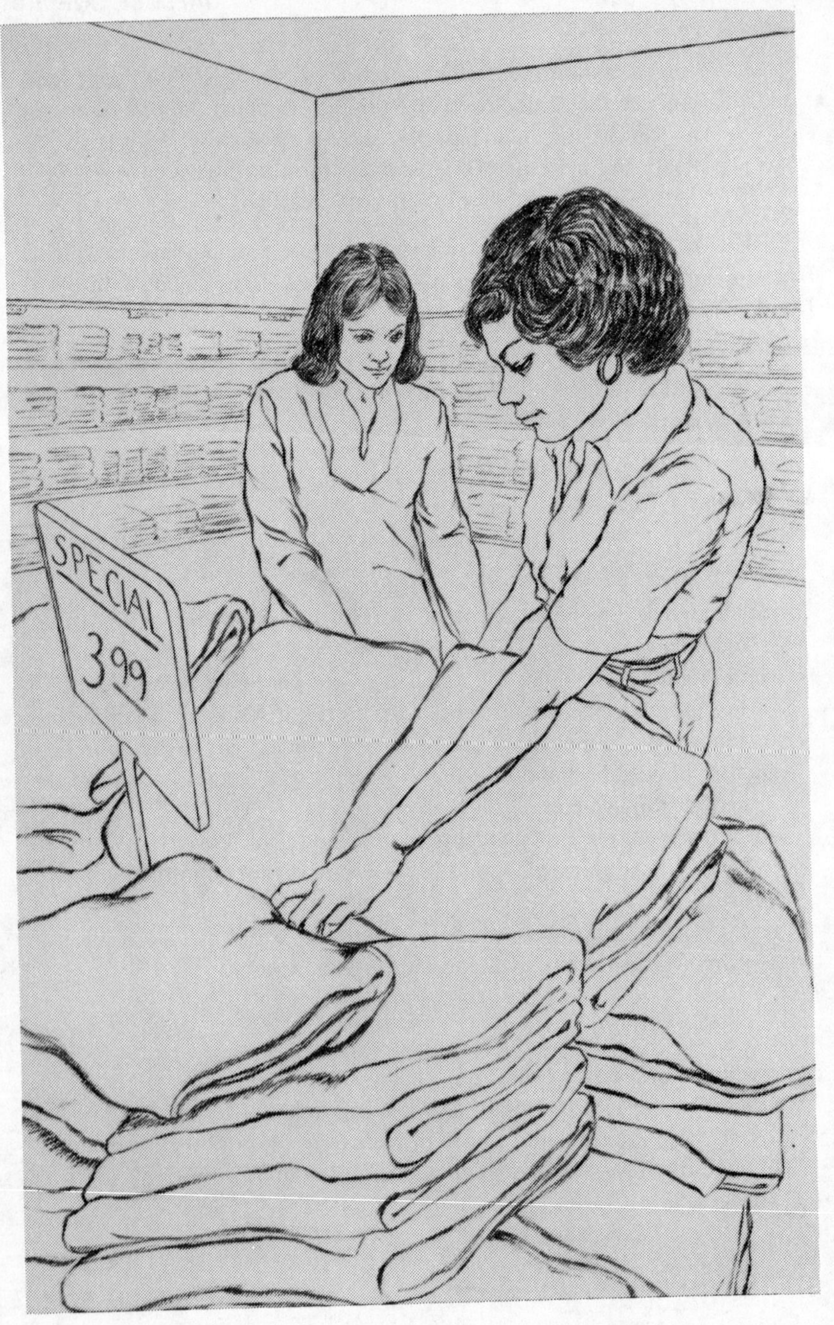
SPECIAL
3.99

CAPSULE TWO

☆ ☆ ☆ ☆ ☆

Woman Alone

DIALOG

[A telephone rings.]

Mary: Hello.

Grace: Hi, Mary, how are you?

Mary: Fine thanks, Grace, and you?

Grace: Trying to beat this heat. What are you doing?

Mary: Not much. I'm trying to catch up on my ironing.

Grace: Today? Well, you are a glutton for punishment. It's going to hit 97° today! I thought you might want to escape the heat and go to the Old Orchard Shopping Center. The stores are all air-conditioned. We can have lunch at Stouffer's. You know they have the "Woman Shopper's Diet Special." And today the August White Sale begins. What do you think?

Mary: You don't have to ask me twice. Great idea! Do you have a babysitter?

Grace: No. My kids are with their grandparents this week.

Mary: Ah! Sweet freedom! Well, let me see if I can line up a sitter. I'll call you right back.

Grace: O.K. Listen, let it ring for a while when you call me back, I may be in the shower. I want to wash my hair.

Mary: O.K. Bye, bye.

[A telephone rings.]

Mrs. Jones: Hello.

Mary: Hi, Mrs. Jones. This is Mary King. Is Karen home? I'd like to go out for a few hours, and I was wondering if she would be able to sit for me.

Mrs. Jones: Just a minute, Mrs. King, I'll call her.

Karen: Hello.

Mary: Hi, Karen. This is Mrs. King. Would you be able to sit for a few hours this afternoon?

Karen: Sure, Mrs. King. I'd love to. What time do you want me to come over?

Mary: How about 11:30? You can give the kids sandwiches for lunch and spend the afternoon in the rubber pool in the backyard.

Karen: Fine! I'll bring my bikini, O.K.?

Mary: Of course. See you at 11:30. Bye, bye.

Karen: Good-bye.

[Two hours later the two women arrive at the parking lot of the Old Orchard Shopping Center.]

Grace: Do you want to shop for a while or are you ready to eat?

Mary: I don't know about you, but I'm starving. It's 12:15! No breakfast this morning. I need some energy to attack the mobs at the sale. Do you feel like eating now?

Grace: Sure! I'm ready. Bring on the "Woman Shopper's Diet Special."

[Once seated in the cool air-conditioned restaurant, the women order their lunch, and their conversation continues.]

Mary: The summer sure slipped right by. I can't believe it's almost time for the kids to go back to school. That will be a relief. Having the three of them at home all day for the entire two and a half months has been too much! You know, I enjoy the role of being a mother, I really do. But the past three months I've felt more like a chauffeur, short-order cook, and valet than a woman realizing herself through the challenging task of motherhood. As soon as the kids are all back in school, I'm going to need a vacation to recuperate from this vacation.

Grace: I know how you feel. What a difference this week was with the boys away visiting their grandparents. I've been getting myself and boys organized to go back to school. Those "Back-to-School" bells are going to ring for me too this year.

Mary: Hey! That's right, you're going to start teaching at the university this fall. I'd forgotten about that. Are you excited about it?

Grace: Excited? I don't know. You know I haven't taught for five years—since my last baby was born. I feel a bit out of touch with today's classroom.

Mary: But you'll get in the swing of things fast. It beats a full-time schedule of diapers, washing and ironing, and tennis lessons on Wednesday afternoons.

Grace: Oh, Mary. The grass is always greener on the other side of the fence. Besides, I'm not working again just to keep from being bored or to give myself something to do. Frankly, Mary, I'm working because I just can't make ends meet on the child support David sends. You know, I didn't ask for alimony.

Mary: Oh, really? No, I wasn't aware of that. Well, since you have an M.A., almost your Ph.D., it would be a little difficult to prove you were incapable of supporting yourself.

Grace: I found that out. I'd really like to be able to study full-time this year and finish my doctorate; but with my going back to teaching and the boys adjusting to living without their father at home, I feel I need to devote as much time as possible to them.

Mary: That's probably wise. How are the boys taking the divorce?

Grace: Fine, I guess. As well as can be expected, under the circumstances. You know, David never actually spent much time at home, what with his traveling and all. So things aren't that different.

Mary: Where's David living?

Grace: He's taken an apartment in the city. The boys spend the weekends with him. They go to museums and the theater and various exhibitions, as well as the aquarium and the planetarium. Culturally it's great for them. Certainly they're seeing more of the city than they used to when weekends meant a barbecue in the backyard.

Mary: So. The boys are adjusting O.K. How about you?

Grace: You know, Mary, I feel relieved and actually excited. The life of the young divorcee is not a bowl of cherries, but I feel like a whole person for the first time since I can remember. Certainly there are more pressures; running a home alone is not easy. But recently I've been painting much more. My studies and my art used to be an escape; now they are an expression of me.

Mary: That's good to hear, Grace. Are you seeing anyone, anyone special, that is?

Grace: Oh, there are several interesting men in my life; but I don't feel that frantic need to "find somebody." I'm really quite content; the boys, my job at the university, my painting—all three offer completely different areas of development in my life. The next time—if there is a next time—I don't think there will be this desperate need to depend on someone.

Mary: Or, in the words of Anaïs Nin, "A joyous encounter of equal force." Hey! Here's our "Diet Special." Let's eat.

COMPREHENSION QUESTIONS

1. Why is Grace going to work at the university this fall?
2. Why is David living in an apartment in the city?
3. How does Grace feel as a result of her divorce?
4. Why does Mary feel relieved that it's almost time for school to begin?
5. What is an August White Sale?
6. What subject does Grace teach?
7. How old do you think the babysitter is?
8. During which months do children normally go to school in the United States? Is it the same in your country?
9. When did Grace quit teaching? Why did she quit?
10. What readjustments are Grace's sons facing at the present?

VOCABULARY

Words Used in Dialog

alimony
August White Sale*
babysitter (sitter)
child support*
desperate
divorce
divorcee
doctorate
encounter
frantic
glutton
incapable
M.A.*
mob
Ph.D.
readjustments
sale
shopping center

Phrases

an expression of me
areas of development
barbecue
bored
bowl of cherries*
glutton for punishment
I'm starving
in the words of

on sale
on the one hand
out of touch with
slipped right by
"taking" (the divorce)*
the grass is always greener . . .
too much
under the circumstances
what with the . . . and all
whole person

Verbs

adjust
beat (the heat)*
catch up on*
depend
devote
escape (the heat)
get in the swing of things
get used to
go out
hit (97°)
line up
make ends meet*
offer
sit (babysit)
take an apartment*
wonder

Slang

bring on the . . . *
it sure beats . . . *

VOCABULARY REVIEW

adjustments	depend	incapable	slipped right by
babysitter	devote	line up	take
beat the heat	glutton	make ends meet	under the circumstances
catch up on	go out	on sale	wonder
child support	in the words of	out of touch with	

A. Fill in the blanks with words or phrases from the vocabulary review above which mean the same as the italicized words in each sentence.

1. When he lost his job, Sam found it difficult to *meet his financial obligations.*
   When he lost his job, San found it difficult ______________.

2. I want *to get appointments for* as many job interviews as possible.
   I want to ______________ as many job interviews as possible.

3. The play was so interesting that time *passed without my noticing it.*
   The play was so interesting that time just ______________.

4. The Joneses can't go tonight because they can't find *a person to watch their baby.*
   The Joneses can't go tonight because they can't find a ______________.

5. I *haven't had any connection with* the educational world for several years.
   I have been ______________ the educational world for several years.

B. Rewrite the following sentences, replacing the italicized word or phrase with one of those listed in the Vocabulary Review above.

1. It's going to be difficult to *make up* all the work you've missed.
2. A divorce requires people to make *many changes* in their lives.
3. She *is curious to know* if you are still interested in the book.
4. She is extremely overweight because she is a *big overeater.*
5. The best time to buy household items is when they are *sold at reduced prices.*

C. Which of the words or phrases listed in the Vocabulary Review above could be used meaningfully in the following sentences?

1. In an effort to ______________ we went to an air-conditioned restaurant and ate ice cream.
2. The dog seems to be ______________ of learning not to jump on the sofa.
3. I'd like to go with you but ______________ I think I'd better visit my sick uncle.
4. In the United States a woman is encouraged to be independent rather than ______________ on someone else for everything.
5. They were so desperate for an apartment that they were willing to ______________ the first one they found.

D. Write an original sentence with each of the following:

1. bring on the
2. to devote

3. frantic
4. on the one hand
5. it sure beats

QUESTIONS FOR DISCUSSION

1. Are Grace and Mary wealthy? Explain your answer. How are their lives different from the lives of women from the same background in your country?
2. Is Grace happy, even though she is divorced? Give evidence to support your answer. Would a divorced woman in your native country feel the same way? Explain.
3. How do Grace and Mary feel about work, children, education, and marriage? Support your ideas with information from the dialog.
4. What is the attitude toward divorced women in your country? What is the attitude there toward divorced men? Is it the same? If not, why do you think there is a difference?
5. How has Women's Liberation influenced the position of women in the United States? What is your definition of a liberated woman? Do you think Grace and/or Mary are examples of liberated women? Why or why not?
6. What does the expression, "The grass is always greener on the other side of the fence" mean? Do you have a similar expression in your native language?
7. Does the "babysitter" exist in your native country? Why or why not? If not, what alternative does your country offer? Would you feel comfortable leaving children with a babysitter? What do you think are the qualities of a good babysitter?

SUGGESTED ACTIVITIES

1. Collect several current articles discussing the various attitudes toward divorce and the readjustment problems of divorced people.
2. Read *Ethan Frome*, a short novel written at the turn of the century by an American woman, Edith Wharton. Report in written or oral form your feelings about the two women in this story.

3. Read *Looking for Mr. Goodbar* by Judith Rossner, a contemporary novel written about a contemporary woman. Report in written or oral form your feelings about the major character.

4. Describe a divorced woman you know in your country or in the United States. How does she support herself and her children, if she has any? What kind of social life does she have?

5. In the United States several groups or organizations have recently developed which have as their purpose to provide a meeting place for parents who are without a partner and are trying to raise children. Write to one of these organizations and ask for literature or information about the group. Report to the class.

GLOSSARY

Vocabulary

alimony—money paid to an ex-mate, usually the husband to the wife. Often paid on a monthly basis for the living expenses of the divorced spouse.

August White Sale—refers to an annual sale of household linens, towels, sheets, etc. Most department stores have them in August and January. They are called White Sales because in the past the majority of these types of items were white.

child support—money paid to an ex-mate, usually the husband to the wife, for the maintenance of the children.

M.A.—a postgraduate degree; usually requires 2 years of additional work after a bachelor's degree.

Ph.D.—a doctoral degree; usually 3 to 5 years of work, including a thesis. Follows the M.A. degree.

Phrases

bowl of cherries—an idiomatic expression meaning that everything's fine.

"taking" (the divorce)—coping with the (divorce or any other) situation.

Verbs

beat (the heat)—overcome or transcend, as opposed to "to defeat" as in a game of cards (he beat me playing cards last night).

catch up on—take advantage of time to do what hasn't been done.

make ends meet—work things out financially and be able to meet all the obligations.
take an apartment—rent an apartment.

Nonstandard English

bring on the—a way of saying, "I can cope with (whatever it is), so let it happen or give it to me."
it sure beats ______________—it's better than ______________.

CAPSULE THREE

A Father's Day Gift

DIALOG

Clerk: Good morning, young ladies, may I help you?

Anne: Yes, thank you. We're buying our father a present for Father's Day.

Clerk: Did you have something special in mind?

Nancy: Maybe a nice necktie, he . . .

Anne: Oh, no, Nancy! People always give their fathers ties for Father's Day, Christmas, birthdays, everything.

Nancy: Okay. I suppose you're right.

Anne: I'd like to look at sports shirts. Something very "in."

Nancy: Oh, yes. Not those conservative styles most of Father's friends wear.

Clerk: What size does your father wear?

Anne: Oh dear. Size? Well, I really don't know. Do you know, Nancy?

Nancy: Gee, I haven't the faintest idea. [To clerk.] But he's about your height and a little heavier.

Clerk: Well, you see our shirts run according to neck size and arm length. For example, 15½/35, 16/34, and so forth.

Anne: Perhaps we should look at something else.

Nancy: Anne, come over here. Look at these pajamas. Aren't they great? The bottoms are just like bermuda shorts. Can't you imagine Father in these?

Anne: They really are terrific. How much do they cost?

Clerk: Indeed. They are very handsome. They are made from imported Italian silk. The price is $45.

Anne and Nancy: Forty-five dollars!

Anne: Forty-five dollars for pajamas, just to sleep in!! Nancy, do you have any other bright ideas?

Nancy: Well, I didn't know the price. And after all, you must admit it was something different.

Anne: For sure! Oh, look at these belts. Aren't they nice leather? I like this one. Feel it, Nancy, it's so soft.

Nancy: Yes, it's really quality leather. But Anne, you know perfectly well that on the inside of Father's closet door he has tons of belts: skinny ones, wide ones, black, brown, tan, canvas.

Anne: That's true, but this is really a super belt.

Clerk: That's the last belt we have left in that particular style. It's a size 32. Do you happen to know what size belt your father wears?

Nancy: Well, not exactly. Mother says he's getting a spare tire.

Clerk: Yes, well, do you have any idea of his waist measurement?

Nancy: Do you see that man over there, Anne?

Anne: You mean the man in the red V-neck sweater?

Nancy: Yes, that one. I think he looks as if he might be about the same size as Father. Why don't we ask him what size he wears and buy that size?

Anne: Oh, Nancy! That man's much fatter than Father. But you were right. The inside of Father's closet door is filled with belts. Maybe we should think about a sweater. Don't they just come small, medium, and large?

Clerk: No, I'm sorry. Our sweaters range from size 36 to size 46. What size do you think your father wears?

Nancy: Excuse me, sir, what size do you wear?

Clerk: Well, I wear a size 38 or 40.

Nancy: Then I think Father wears a 42.

Anne: Oh, no, Nancy. I think Father must wear a 44.

Clerk: Have you girls considered a nice bathrobe? They come in sizes small, medium, and large. We have a handsome terrycloth robe that is on sale this week.

Anne: But I think Mother is going to buy him a new robe, isn't she, Nancy?

Nancy: I think that's what she said. Socks. What about socks? Let's buy Father some socks. Hey! Look who's here. Eva Bloom. Hi, Eva.

Eva: Hi, Nancy. Imagine bumping into you here. What are you doing?

Nancy: My sister and I are buying our father a Father's Day present. Have you met my sister, Anne?

Eva: No, I haven't.

Nancy: Eva, this is Anne. Anne, Eva Bloom. We're in the same algebra class.

Anne: Hi, Eva, nice to meet you. I've heard Nancy mention your name every time she gets stuck on an algebra problem.

Eva: And I've heard all about your winning the Junior High School Science Award! Congratulations.

Anne: Thanks! Are you here buying a Fathers' Day present too?

Eva: No, we always just give Father and Mother breakfast in bed. And then for dinner, we take him to his favorite restaurant. I mean it's impossible to buy him something; he has everything.

Nancy: That seems to be our problem too.

Clerk: Uh-hum!

Anne: Oh, excuse us. We haven't forgotten. Let's see, where were we?

Clerk: I believe the last item to be considered was socks.

Eva: Well, excuse me, I must be going. See you Monday in algebra, Nancy. Nice meeting you, Anne.

Nancy: Bye, bye. See you Monday.

Anne: Nice to meet you too, Eva.

Clerk: Uh-hum! Now then, would you like to see some socks?

Anne: But Nancy, Father has a drawer full of socks. And what size shoe does he take? I think he has rather large feet, but I don't know what size.

Nancy: Neither do I. Oh, Anne. Look at this beautiful leather jacket. Wouldn't he look smart in this? I wish we had the money to buy this for Father.

Anne: Well, we could charge it.

Nancy: But since Father pays the bill, it would hardly be like a gift, would it?

Anne: Oh, what are we going to do? It's getting late.

Clerk: Have you young ladies thought about a gift certificate from the store. Then your father could choose his own gift.

Anne: But that's like giving money. I'd much rather pick out something especially for him.

Nancy: Me too.

Clerk: Well then, what about a nice tie? We have some lovely imported ties. And there's just one size in ties.

Anne: Hey, that's a great idea!

Nancy: Why didn't we think of that before?

COMPREHENSION QUESTIONS

1. Why were Anne and Nancy buying their father a present?
2. What was their first idea for a gift? Why didn't they buy it?

Gift Certificate
No. 49
This Certificate Entitles
Dollars
To Select a Gift In the Amount of
Presented by
By
Amount $
Date
H. G. Lamb Co.
437 Washington Street
Eugene, Oregon

CHARGE ACCOUNT APPLICATION **PLEASE ANSWER ALL QUESTIONS**	☐	R.C.	APPROVED BY

IMPORTANT: CHECK THOSE BLOCKS BELOW THAT APPLY OR APPLICATION CANNOT BE PROCESSED.

☐ **Individual Account**—Applicant is relying on his/her income and assets and credit references provided below – Complete sections 1, 2 and 3.

☐ You must check this block if spouse will use this account and state spouse's name: ______________________
spouse's name

NOTE: PAYMENTS FROM ALIMONY, CHILD SUPPORT OR MAINTENANCE NEED NOT BE REPORTED AS INCOME UNLESS YOU ARE RELYING ON SUCH PAYMENTS IN THIS APPLICATION.

❷ **INDIVIDUAL INFORMATION (ALL APPLICANTS)**

YOUR NAME — FIRST / INITIAL / LAST			NO. OF DEPENDENTS
YOUR SOCIAL SECURITY NO	AREA CODE	PHONE NO. AT ADDRESS	☐ OWN HOME ☐ BOARD W/PARENTS ☐ RENT ☐ MOBILE HOME
YOUR PRESENT ADDRESS — STREET			MO. MTGE./RENT
CITY / STATE		ZIP CODE	HOW LONG
YOUR FORMER ADDRESS (IF LESS THAN 3 YEARS AT PRESENT ADDRESS)			HOW LONG
I AM EMPLOYED BY (GIVE FULL NAME)		POSITION	HOW LONG
BUSINESS ADDRESS		BUS. PHONE	WEEKLY SALARY
YOUR FORMER EMPLOYER		POSITION	HOW LONG
MY BANK ACCOUNT IS AT		AMOUNT AND SOURCE OF OTHER INCOME. SEE SECTION ① ABOVE.	
BRANCH ADDRESS		☐ CHECK ☐ SAVING ☐ LOAN	ARE YOU 18 OR OVER ☐ YES ☐ NO
NEAREST RELATIVE NOT LIVING WITH YOU	NAME ADDRESS		PHONE NO.

❸ PLEASE LIST NAMES OF STORES FINANCE COMPANIES OTHER CREDIT CARDS AND ALSO INDICATE AMOUNT OWING AND ACCOUNT NUMBER OF CREDIT REFERENCE GIVEN.

NAME OF STORE OR BUSINESS	NAME UNDER WHICH ACCOUNT IS HELD	AMOUNT OWING	ACCOUNT NUMBER

SIGNATURE OF APPLICANT ______________________ DATE __________

Any holder of this consumer credit contract is subject to all claims and defenses which the debtor could assert against the seller of goods or services obtained pursuant hereto or with the proceeds hereof. Recovery hereunder by the debtor shall not exceed amounts paid by the debtor hereunder.

3. Why didn't the girls buy the pajamas?
4. What does Eva give her father for Father's Day?
5. Why did the two girls decide not to charge the gift they were buying?
6. What is a gift certificate?
7. What did the two girls finally decide to buy?
8. How does Nancy know Eva?
9. Why didn't the girls buy a belt?
10. What was the girls' mother planning to buy their father?

VOCABULARY

Words Used in Dialog

bathrobe (robe)
bottoms
closet
conservative
gift certificate
handsome
imported
leather
measurement
price
selection
silk
size
skinny
style
sweater
terrycloth

Phrases

bump into (a person)*
faintest idea*
on sale
something special in mind
where were we?*

Verbs

charge it
choose
come (in sizes)*
consider
get stuck on*
look smart*
pick out
range (in size)*
run (in size)*
take (a size)*
wear

Slang

"in"*
gee
spare tire*

VOCABULARY REVIEW

bumped into	gift certificate	range (in size)	spare tire
charge it	handsome	select	take (size)
closet	look smart	selection	faintest idea
conservative	measurement	something special in mind	wear
consider	on sale		where were we?

A. Which of the words or phrases listed in the Vocabulary Review above could be used meaningfully in the following sentences?

1. I really want to buy that record, but I don't have any money with me. Perhaps I should ____________.
2. I haven't the ____________ what to give my boss for Christmas.
3. This store has a wide ____________ of gift items.
4. My brother isn't exactly overweight, but he has a ____________.
5. She hadn't seen Robert for ages when she ____________ him at the theater.
6. Let's see, ____________ when I was called to the phone?
7. A basic black dress and pearls always ____________ for a formal occasion.
8. Her little brother helped Inga ____________ the gift for their parents' anniversary.
9. In that store the shoes ____________ from 2½ to 11!
10. When you give a ____________ you know that the person will select what he wants.

Use each group of words and phrases in the given order, and form them to make an original and meaningful sentence.

Example: store / sells / wide range
This store sells a wide range of gifts and crafts.

1. sweaters / run / sizes / small, medium, large
2. range / sizes

3. brother / picked out / bathrobe / present
4. chose / birthday gift / charged
5. imported ties / come / wide variety of colors

C. Write an original sentence with each of the following:

1. bumped into
2. conservative
3. something special in mind
4. get stuck on
5. pick out

QUESTIONS FOR DISCUSSION

1. What are the advantages/disadvantages of giving someone a gift certificate for a present? Do you enjoy this type of gift? Is it more appropriate in some situations than in others?
2. Do you think the two sisters were well-mannered? Do you think they come from a well-educated family? Why or why not? Do you think they come from a very wealthy family? Support your opinion with evidence from the dialog.
3. Describe a gift-buying situation in your native country. Discuss the similarities and differences with the scene you have just read and listened to.
4. How did the clerk treat the girls? Was he patient or impatient? Rude or polite? Why did he behave as he did? How might he behave during the Christmas season or on other specific gift-buying days? Have you ever worked as a clerk? If so, what experiences have you had?
5. Is Father's Day celebrated in your native country? If so, how is it celebrated? What differences, if any, are there in the way Mother's Day is celebrated in your native country, and the way Father's Day is celebrated?
6. How is Christmas (New Year's, Independence Day) celebrated in your native country? What date is celebrated? In what manner is the day celebrated?

SUGGESTED ACTIVITIES

1. From current United States newspapers collect an assortment of advertisements announcing various clothing items on sale. Write a report in which you describe what can be found on sale and where it can be found.

2. It's not always easy to buy a gift for someone. Share with the class an experience you've had trying to select an appropriate Christmas gift, birthday gift, anniversary gift, etc.

3. With several other members of the class, prepare a mini-drama in which you and a friend are shopping together and you run into your teacher or a friend of yours or your parents. You must make the necessary introductions.

4. With several other members of the class, prepare a mini-drama in which you and a friend are at a cocktail party. You suddenly find yourselves with two young married couples, both of whom you know, but neither of whom knows the other. Make the necessary introductions.

5. If you are living in the United States, find out what are the working hours of the department stores, banks, supermarkets, dry cleaners, and shopping centers in the area where you live. Report to the class.

6. Write a composition in which you describe a typical gift-buying situation in your native country. Or, compare gift buying in your native country with gift buying in the United States. Include such information as where you buy the gift, how it is gift-wrapped, how it is given to the person, when it should be opened, and what is considered an appropriate gift for this particular occasion.

7. You have been in the hospital for two weeks. Your boss at work sent you a book (or flowers or candy) as a gift while you were in the hospital. Write him or her a thank you note.

GLOSSARY

Phrases

bump into (a person)—not really physically touching someone, but to encounter someone by accident. Also used: *run into.*

faintest idea—to have no idea with regard to something.
where were we?—what were we talking about or doing when we were interrupted?

Verbs

come (in sizes)—the different sizes available.
get stuck on—have difficulty with.
look smart—look stylish or fashionable.
range (in size)—from the smallest to the largest.
run (in size)—how size is classified for a particular item of clothing.
take (size)—the size you wear.

Nonstandard English

"in"—popular or fashionable.
spare tire—roll of fat around the waist.

VOCABULARY REVIEW, CAPSULES 1 to 3

to afford
to assume
August White Sale
avenue
babysitter
boulevard
to bump into
to charge it
clustered around
commuting
conservative
cosmopolitan
cracking down
to enforce
expressway
gift certificate
high-rise apartments
jaywalking
trying to make ends meet
out of touch
range
rush hour
shopping centers
touchy business
urban renewal

Which of the words or phrases listed above could be used meaningfully in the following sentences? It may be necessary to make changes in the forms of the words.

1. When people travel back and forth to work every day, from the suburbs to downtown, or from downtown to the suburbs, it is called ________________.

2. Crossing the street in the middle of the block is illegal and is called ______________.

3. A road that cuts through the city from one end to another, without traffic lights, is called an ______________.

4. Many large old homes are being torn down and replaced by modern ______________.

5. Heavy traffic during the morning and afternoon hours is called ______________.

6. Downtown commercial areas are rapidly being replaced by large clusters of stores in outlying suburban areas called ______________.

7. Every year in the late summer, household towels and linens go on sale at reduced prices during what is known as an ______________.

8. The struggle to meet financial demands of day-to-day living is often referred to as ______________.

9. A person who comes into the home on an hourly basis for the sole purpose of watching children while the parents are away is called a ______________.

10. Someone who hasn't been in contact with a specific field of thought over an extended period of time is said to be ______________.

11. A subtle way of giving a cash gift is in the form of a ______________.

12. A convenient way to pay for a purchase when you have no cash is ______________.

13. If a store has a wide selection of merchandise, you might also say that they have a wide ______________ of merchandise.

14. A dark suit and a white shirt and tie would be considered the ______________ look for men.

15. If by chance you meet someone, you might say that you ______________ them.

CAPSULE FOUR

Eating Right

DIALOG

Judy: Well, Marjorie, this is a pleasant surprise. It seems to me we ran into each other here last week too.

Marjorie: You and I must have the same idea, Judy. The only way to beat the crowds when you do the grocery shopping on Saturday is to be here when they open at 9:00 sharp!

Judy: Right you are! Look at this fruit! Ummmmm! But can you believe the price of a pint of red raspberries? There goes my idea of raspberry pancakes for Sunday breakfast.

Marjorie: But don't they look delicious? Guess this weekend my family will have to settle for cold watermelon or fresh peaches and sugar.

Judy: Marjorie, have you ever been to the fresh fruit and vegetable market on Highway 67? Their produce is so much more reasonably priced, and everything is farm-fresh.

Marjorie: Yes, I drove out there once with Kay Clemens. They have lovely stuff. And the prices are excellent. But this supermarket is so close to home, and I'm a creature of comfort.

Judy: Aren't we all? Oh would you look at those enormous cucumbers! I think I'll make pickles next week. I've been trying, as much as possible, to stay away from preserved foods; but it's not always easy in this plastic-oriented society.

Marjorie: Well, this is one preserved food that my family can't live without: peanut butter. Would you believe we go through a jar every week?

Judy: Peanut butter and jelly sandwiches. They are as American as apple pie.

Marjorie: Speaking of apple pie, if you're ever in a pinch, these frozen pies are really tasty. I always keep a couple on hand for whenever the kids invite unexpected friends over for the afternoon.

Judy: That's a good idea. But right now, since I'm trying to stress good eating, and natural, unpreserved foods, I can just hear my family, "Oh, Mom! This pie is pure plastic." I forgot to put dog food on my list; how lucky I saw this. We're completely out! I need both the canned dog food and a twenty-five-pound bag of the dry food. As you can see, our dogs are not included in the natural foods–not yet, that is!

Marjorie: From the way you're buying, I assume you didn't ride your bike here today.

Judy: You're absolutely right! Jane, my older daughter, had her new ten-speed bicycle stolen last Tuesday.

Marjorie: Oh, no! How?

Judy: Well, when she came home from school, she left it unlocked in the backyard. She came into the house just long enough to change her clothes and call a friend. When she went out fifteen minutes later, the bike was gone.

Marjorie: What a shame! You know, this neighborhood just isn't as secure as it used to be.

Judy: That's no excuse. We tell the kids always to lock their bikes. But I guess experience is the best teacher. So today she borrowed my bike to go on a Girl Scout bike hike! I'm going to take advantage of the station wagon and really stock up.

Marjorie: My, this natural foods section is certainly growing. I didn't know half these foods existed! I've tried this granola cereal. Have you? It's not only healthful but very good. And fattening, too, I might add.

Judy: I bought some boxes of granola at the Natural Food Store on Market Street several months ago. Then Jane and Sarah started making their own recipe for granola, although recently the novelty of that has worn off. Perhaps I'll try this brand, since you recommend it. Oh, here are the spices. I need some vanilla extract and oregano. I've been trying to grow most of my spices in the garden. If you need any dill or parsley, come on over.

Marjorie: Thanks, I just might take you up on that. Oh! Will you look at all those imported cheeses? Fred and the boys have recently become very big on cheese. Last month we went to Wisconsin to spend two weeks with my parents. We came home with practically half our luggage filled with different cheeses. Now I'm afraid my family is spoiled. I was making cheese sauces to go with broccoli, cauliflower, spinach, everything. Suddenly vegetables were very popular at my house.

Judy: Here's that new low-calorie cola drink that's been advertised everywhere for the past two months. They have great TV commercials. Have you tried it yet?

Marjorie: No, but I think I will. Warm weather makes me so thirsty. Have you tried this brand of diet ice cream? It's very tasty. I gave it to the kids once and they never even noticed the difference.

Judy: Combine the two. Diet cola over diet ice cream for the "Gourmet Dieters' Delight." Perfect for that sizzling summer afternoon.

Marjorie: You sound like a TV commercial. Look at this!! Can you believe these meat prices? It certainly forces you to be creative. I think I'll publish the new best seller: *One Hundred and One Ways to Cook Hamburger—in Disguise.*

Judy: Would you believe that both my daughters, Jane and Sarah, have been vegetarians for the past two and a half months, ever since Jane studied nutrition in the Girl Scouts. So I've just been purchasing meat for Phil and myself, and I've been cooking a lot of fish. It's really not any cheaper, but Jane is convinced that red meat is bad for human beings. I wonder how long this phase will last.

Marjorie: Well, with the four boys and Fred, I have to cook meat every night. But in the summer we cook out almost every evening. The boys love it; they take turns playing chef. And even hamburger tastes better when it's cooked on a grill. Oh! which reminds me, I forgot to get a bag of charcoal. Will you watch my cart here in line? I'll be back in a jiffy!

COMPREHENSION QUESTIONS

1. Why did the women go shopping so early on Saturday morning?
2. Why was Jane's bicycle stolen?
3. Why did Judy offer Marjorie fresh spices?
4. Why didn't Judy follow Marjorie's suggestion to stock up on frozen pies?

5. Why has Marjorie been cooking with a lot of cheese recently?
6. Why has Judy been cooking a lot of fish lately?
7. What did Judy call a "Gourmet Dieters' Delight"?
8. Why did Judy come shopping in the station wagon?
9. Why have Judy's two daughters recently become vegetarians?
10. Why don't the two women buy their produce at the fresh fruit market on the highway?

VOCABULARY

Words Used in Dialog

bags
brand
broccoli
cans
cart
cauliflower
charcoal
chef
crowds
cucumbers
dill
dog food
extract
fattening
frozen
granola*
grocery
healthful
imported
jar
jelly
oregano
outdoors
parsley
peaches
peanut butter
phase
pickles
produce
raspberries
sauce
shopping
sizzling
spices
tasty
vegetarians

Phrases

come on over
creature of comfort*
experience is the best teacher
farm-fresh
in a pinch*
low-calorie
novelty has worn off
pleasant surprise
preserved food
reasonably priced
right you are
take turns
very big on*
what a shame
would you believe

Verbs

assume
beat (the crowd)*
borrow
cook out
keep on hand*
recommend
run into (person)*
run out of
settle for
stay (away from)
steal
stress
stock up on*
take advantage of
take you up on (something)*
wonder

Slang

sharp!
in a jiffy*

VOCABULARY REVIEW

borrow
come on over
extract
in a jiffy
in a pinch
keep on hand
noncalorie
pleasant surprise
recommend
run into
run out of
sharp
sizzling
stay away from
stock up on
take turns
took her up on
vegetarians
very big on
what a shame

A. Rewrite each sentence substituting words or phrases from the Vocabulary Review above for the italicized words.

1. What an *unexpected pleasure* to meet you here!
2. *In an emergency*, you can count on me.
3. This is a good cola, and it *has few calories.*
4. I always like to *have* ice cream *available* in case of unexpected visitors.
5. I *met* her *unexpectedly* yesterday.
6. Whenever there's a sale, I *buy a lot of* coffee.
7. I'll be there *immediately.*
8. I try to *avoid* crowds.
9. I *accepted* her offer to have a cup of tea.
10. *How sad* that your favorite team lost!

B. Choose the correct word form to fit into each sentence.

1. *taste, to taste, tasty, tastily, tasted*
   a. I like the ________ of cauliflower.
   b. The fish was ________ prepared.
   c. We ________ the cheese, and it wasn't fresh.
   d. We enjoyed the ________ hamburgers.
   e. I like ________ the different kinds of wines at wine-tasting parties.

2. *wonder, to wonder, wonderful, wonderfully, wondered*
   a. He is a ________ husband.
   b. There is no need ________ where the money is coming from.
   c. The music was performed ________.
   d. She ________ out loud about what had happened.
   e. The comic strip character, ________ Woman, has become very popular.

3. *steal, to steal, stolen, stole, steals*
   a. This coat is a ________ at $49.95.
   b. Someone ________ the jewels last night.
   c. The ________ painting was returned.
   d. He tried ________ my wife, so I shot him.
   e. Who ________ my purse ________ trash. (Shakespeare.)

4. *fish, to fish, fishy, fished*
   a. His story sounded very ________.
   b. They go out ________ every Sunday.
   c. That's the biggest ________ story I've ever heard.
   d. They ________ all night and didn't catch a thing.
   e. This food has a ________ taste.

5. *produce, to produce, produced, production*
   a. Most countries prefer ________ as much as possible.
   b. Sugar is a major ________ of many Latin American nations.

c. A country that ______________ less than it needs has a serious problem.

d. The ______________ of cars in the United States has increased over the years.

e. Last year the United States ______________ more goods that the year before.

C. Read the following short paragraph. When you have finished, close your book and try to write the paragraph from memory. The instructor will have a list of guide words on the blackboard to help you.

When you shop for produce in the country, you usually find things reasonably priced. It's often a pleasant surprise to come upon farm-fresh eggs for thirty cents a dozen less than the price in the city. So instead of settling for stale and expensive supermarket food, take advantage of the good weather and drive out to the country to do your shopping.

QUESTIONS FOR DISCUSSION

1. On a scale of one to ten, with one representing "poor" and ten representing "wealthy," how would you rate Judy and Marjorie? Support your answer with information from the dialog.

2. What effects did the Girl Scouts have on Judy's daughter? How did this influence the family? Do you think this is good or bad? Are there similar youth groups in your country?

3. What is the difference in the nutritional value of food bought in the rural areas and in the large cities? What are the advantages and disadvantages of shopping in each of these places?

4. Compare shopping in a United States supermarket with the way people normally shop in your native country. Are there any supermarkets in your native country? If so, compare them with the ones you have seen in the United States or the one described in the dialog.

5. Judy is obviously interested in the current trend toward natural foods. What do you know about this? Do you eat any natural or diet foods? Which ones? Why?

6. People in the United States have been severely criticized for extensive waste. Do you think this criticism is justified? Give reasons and examples. Is there waste in your native country?

SUGGESTED ACTIVITIES

1. Collect several recent newspaper and magazine articles which discuss current trends in modern supermarket or trends in nutrition. In an oral or written project, report the results of your investigation.
2. Write a description of a supermarket or food store that you often shop in. Describe the smells, colors, shapes, sounds, the people who work and shop there, the way products are arranged, how you pay for your purchases.
3. In a composition, contrast the streamlined modern supermarket with the grocery store of the past. Compare the way the food is displayed, the manner of pricing articles to be sold, the different means of transporting food to the place of sale, hygiene, etc.
4. The United States has been called "the most overfed and undernourished nation." What do you think is meant by that statement? Do you think it is a valid criticism? Explain your ideas to the class and use examples to support your opinions.
5. Read one of the books written by Adele Davis in which she discusses the importance of proper diet. Which ideas do you agree with and disagree with? Explain.

GLOSSARY

Vocabulary

granola—a cereal made from whole grains and dried fruits; there are no preservatives added. There are commercially made granola cereals, or it can be made at home.

Phrases

creature of comfort—a phrase often used to describe a member of the well-off, comfortable, gadget-oriented, middle-class United States society.

in a pinch—at a difficult moment; in an emergency.
very big on—like a great deal.

Verbs

beat (the crowd)—to avoid; as in "to beat the heat" (capsule 2).
keep on hand—have available.
run into—not actually hit, but accidentally encounter; *bump into* (capsule 3).
stock up on—buy a lot of staple items.
take you up on—do as someone has suggested.

Nonstandard English

in a jiffy—very quickly.

CAPSULE FIVE

Living in a Loft

DIALOG

[A telephone rings.]

Sandy: Good afternoon, Toro-Import. May I help you? Yes, one moment, please. Mr. Kaplin. Telephone, line one.

[She continues typing; the telephone rings again.]

Sandy: Good afternoon, Toro . . . Oh! Hi, Ben. How are you? Is he really? Terrific! Okay, fine. I'll meet you both at the White Horse at 5:45. Afterwards we can go to the loft. Right! See you there.

[At 5:00 Sandy leaves the office, catches the crosstown bus to the subway, takes the A train to 18th Street, where she gets off and walks three blocks to an English pub on the corner. She walks in.]

Ben: Sandy! Here we are. Over here in the corner.

[Sandy walks to the table; she sits down, bubbling with excitement and says]

Sandy: Hey! What's happening, Jon? When did you get in? You look great!

Jon: About six hours ago. Thanks. So do you. What's with the fancy clothes? Are your blue jeans dirty?

Sandy: No! It's my new gig. I'm working a real J-O-B! I'm a receptionist at an import company. Somehow levis and a paint-splattered work shirt just don't make it uptown.

Ben: Right! So she divided her first month's salary between Lord & Taylor and Bloomingdale's for an entire new wardrobe. Can you believe that?

Sandy: Hey! I didn't come here to talk about my new clothes. I want to hear about Guatemala. And the movie. How's the movie? Did you sell it?

Jon: Not yet! But I think it's going to make it! Siegal is very interested. I called him when I got in this afternoon. I'm seeing him first thing at 9:30 tomorrow morning. Want some wine? We ordered an extra glass for you. Or would you prefer something else?

Sandy: Wine sounds fine. It'll take the edge off a rough day at work. So you're going to see Siegal tomorrow. Fantastic! He's got to accept it. There's not another film like it, I'm sure. And Guatemala? How was it? Tell me everything!

Jon: Guatemala is like nothing you can imagine. Remember when we went to Oaxaca?

Ben: Remember? Will we ever forget? One VW camper, two dogs, four human beings, and 102° in the shade. And those mountains from Oaxaca to Tehuantepec . . . I'll never forget them.

Jon: Well, multiply that whole trip by three and you've got Guatemala. The people are so uncomplicated and beautiful. And the arts and crafts are incredible! Such colors! Such design! Such creativity!

Sandy: Oh, Ben, I want to go! Ben, do you think after this copy of your thesis is handed in we can go? This city is stifling. It seems forever that I've been sitting here in New York City, wasting my life away.

Ben: Forever, the little woman says. It's March and as I do recall we spent October, November, and December in sunny California. Would you like that last exaggerated complaint stricken from the record?

Sandy: But Berkeley doesn't count! You were doing research in graduate school and I was working so hard on my final exhibition.

Jon: Hey! Your exhibition!! I almost forgot. How was it? Are you the budding young artist about to bloom?

Ben: Bloom? Man, she has blossomed! Would you believe that before you sits an artist who sold 17 of her 21 pieces which were exhibited in December? And you should have read the reviews. The critics loved her. Not only did she make it into the regular university paper and the local periodicals, but there was a full-page spread in the *San Francisco Gazette.*

Jon: That's fine! Really fine!! So, what's with this import company job?

Sandy: True, I sold seventeen paintings, but I had no idea of the expense involved with putting together an exhibition. And my prices aren't exactly in Picasso's range, you know. At least, not yet. And I had to pay back my school loans for undergraduate school. Then we bought a van to drive here. Well, let me tell you, Jon, it's very expensive living in this big, fancy city.

Ben: To further complicate matters, my grant wasn't renewed for January. So we've been living off the earnings of "Big Mama" here! But in June everything will be smooth. They've given me an assistantship at the university beginning the summer quarter.

Jon: When do you think you'll be through with this Nobel Prize winning research? Or shouldn't I ask?

Ben: Right, man. Better not ask! Actually, with the assistantship I hope I can finish after the first of the year and have my Ph.D. before June. But then you never know for sure! I still have to take my doctoral comprehensive.

Jon: Where are you two living in this big, ugly city?

Sandy: Oh, it's great, Jon, just great. We found a loft. It's in the old industrial part of town. We rented the entire second floor for $170 a month. It used to be a warehouse for men's underwear. Is that status?

Ben: It's a cross between living in a roller rink and the Roman Coliseum. You know, small, cozy, and intimate.

Sandy: Listen to him!!! You love it and you know it. Jon, you should see how Ben fixed it up. We bought a huge potbelly stove at an auction. I actually can cook on it. Ben opened two fireplaces in the walls and built a large loft overhanging one end. That's where we sleep. Downstairs my studio is at the far end and . . . but why am I sitting here describing it? Let's go home and you can see it.

Jon: Do you still make that dynamite stuffed eggplant?

Ben: Does she! The truth is, Jon, I've been calling her Julia Child lately when she's in the kitchen. This woman is not-to-be-believed on her potbelly stove.

Sandy: Okay. Okay. Flattery will get you everywhere. I can see it now. Stuffed eggplant for three—coming up.

COMPREHENSION QUESTIONS

1. Using information in the dialog, describe Sandy's job.
2. What was Jon doing in Guatemala?
3. Why had Sandy bought some new clothes recently?
4. Where did the three friends meet for drinks? What kind of place was it?
5. How have Ben and Sandy been supporting themselves for the last several months?
6. Describe the place where Ben and Sandy live.
7. What does Sandy do in addition to her job?
8. Using information in the dialog, describe Ben's work.
9. Where were Ben and Sandy before they came to New York? What did they do there?
10. Using information from the dialog, describe the trip that Ben and Sandy took to Oaxaca.

VOCABULARY

Words Used in Dialog

assistantship
auction
cozy
creativity
critics
earnings
exhibition
fireplace
flattery
graduate school
grant
intimate
loans
loft
overhanging
periodicals
Ph.D.
quarter
receptionist
reviews
shade
status
thesis
undergraduate school
underwear
untarnished
uptown
wardrobe
warehouse

Phrases

bubbling with excitement*
budding young artist*
coming right up*
doctoral comprehensives
first thing in the morning
full-page spread*
paint-splattered
potbelly stove*
price range
roller rink
stricken from the record*
wasting my life away

Verbs

be through
bloom*
blossom
catch (a bus)*
complicate
fix up
hand in
live off*
prefer
stifle
take (a train)*
take the edge off*

Slang

catch you later*
dynamite* (adjective)
gig*
make it*
man*
not-to-be-believed*
smooth
what's happening?
what's with . . . ?

VOCABULARY REVIEW

be through	make it
bloom	overhanging
bubbling with excitement	paint-splattered
catch you later	potbelly
complicate	prefer to
critics	price range
expensive	smooth
fix up	status
hand in	take (a train or bus)
is coming right up	take the edge off

A. Rewrite the following sentences, replacing the italicized portion with words or phrases from the Vocabulary Review above.

1. Every morning I have to *catch* the 7:05 bus in order to arrive on time at the office.
2. If you continue to drink so much beer, you're going to have a *big stomach* within a very short time.
3. She has a great ability to *decorate* old houses.
4. You must *give* your report to the boss before Thursday.
5. The food *will be ready in just a minute.*
6. Why don't you eat an apple to *take away* your appetite until we have dinner?
7. It seems that manual only *makes* things *more difficult.*
8. Your jeans are really *covered with paint.*
9. He was *full of enthusiasm* after he won the tennis match.
10. I'd *rather* go to the opera than sit home and watch television.

B. Which of the words or phrases listed in the Vocabulary Review above could be meaningfully used in the following sentences?

1. That car is really too expensive, it's way beyond our ______________.
2. A cup of tea usually ______________ my hunger.

3. The ______________ balcony gives the room a larger appearance.
4. ______________ in the morning papers gave the movie a good review.
5. I don't get much salary, but I like the job because there is a lot of ______________ connected with it.

C. Write an original sentence for each of the following:

1. What's with
2. Make it
3. Take the edge off
4. Live off
5. Smooth (as an adjective in idiomatic slang)

QUESTIONS FOR DISCUSSION

1. Would Sandy and Ben have any difficulty getting a bank loan or credit cards? Explain your answer.
2. Sandy and Ben are both living off Sandy's income right now. If you were Sandy/Ben, would this bother you? Defend your position.
3. Do you think Sandy and Ben are married? What makes you think as you do?
4. What do you think about two people living together without being married? What are some disadvantages and advantages? Why do most societies disapprove of this kind of arrangement?
5. In your native country are there many young people, married or unmarried, living as Sandy and Ben do? If not, why do you think not?

6. Do you believe that a "woman's place is in the home"? Explain. Next to each of the following jobs, write *male, female,* or *both,* depending on who you think is best suited to do them. Give reasons for your answers.

   child raising
   being an executive
   cooking
   house cleaning
   driving a taxi
   teaching
   tailoring

7. The expression is, "Flattery will get you nowhere." Why do you think Sandy purposely misquoted the expression? Which of the two versions do you think is more often true? Why? Is there such an expression in your native language?

8. Who do you think paid the bill when Sandy, Ben, and Jon left the pub? Explain your answer. If the bill was $7.80, what kind of tip should have been left?

SUGGESTED ACTIVITIES

1. From current English language newspapers and magazines collect several articles which discuss changing roles among married and unmarried people in different countries.

2. With another member of the class prepare a short mini-drama in which a young man and a young woman from the same office are having a drink after work. When the bill comes, the young man is away from the table making a phone call; so she goes ahead and pays the bill. What happens when he comes back to the table?

3. Which of the following do you think causes the most trouble between couples in your native country and in the United States? Discuss with the class.

   money
   the husband watching a football game on TV
   educational differences
   a night out "with the boys"
   the woman wanting (not wanting) to work (study)

4. Explain orally, or in writing, why you could or could not comfortably accept the roles assumed by Ben/Sandy.

5. Write a brief composition on the Nobel Prize. In what year was it first begun? In what country was it originated? In what specific areas is the prize granted? Has anyone from your native country ever won the Nobel Prize? If so, who and for what?

6. Write a composition in which you defend your feelings about why couples should or should not live together without being married.

GLOSSARY

Phrases

bubbling with excitement—filled with enthusiasm.
budding young artist—a beginner with good potential.
coming right up—it will be ready soon.
full-page spread—a newspaper story covering an entire page.
potbelly stove—a circular stove which burns wood or coal (resembles a protruding stomach).
stricken from the record—a legal term meaning not to be officially recorded (used humorously in nonlegal situations).

Verbs

bloom—realize one's ambitions.
catch (a bus)—travel by.
live off—live on someone else's earnings.
take (a train)—travel by.

Nonstandard English

dynamite—an adjective to mean incredible.
gig—job.
make it—in this case it means to be acceptable.
man—an affectionate and commonly used term for a friend—as *baby* for a woman.
not-to-be-believed—a term of high praise, incredible.

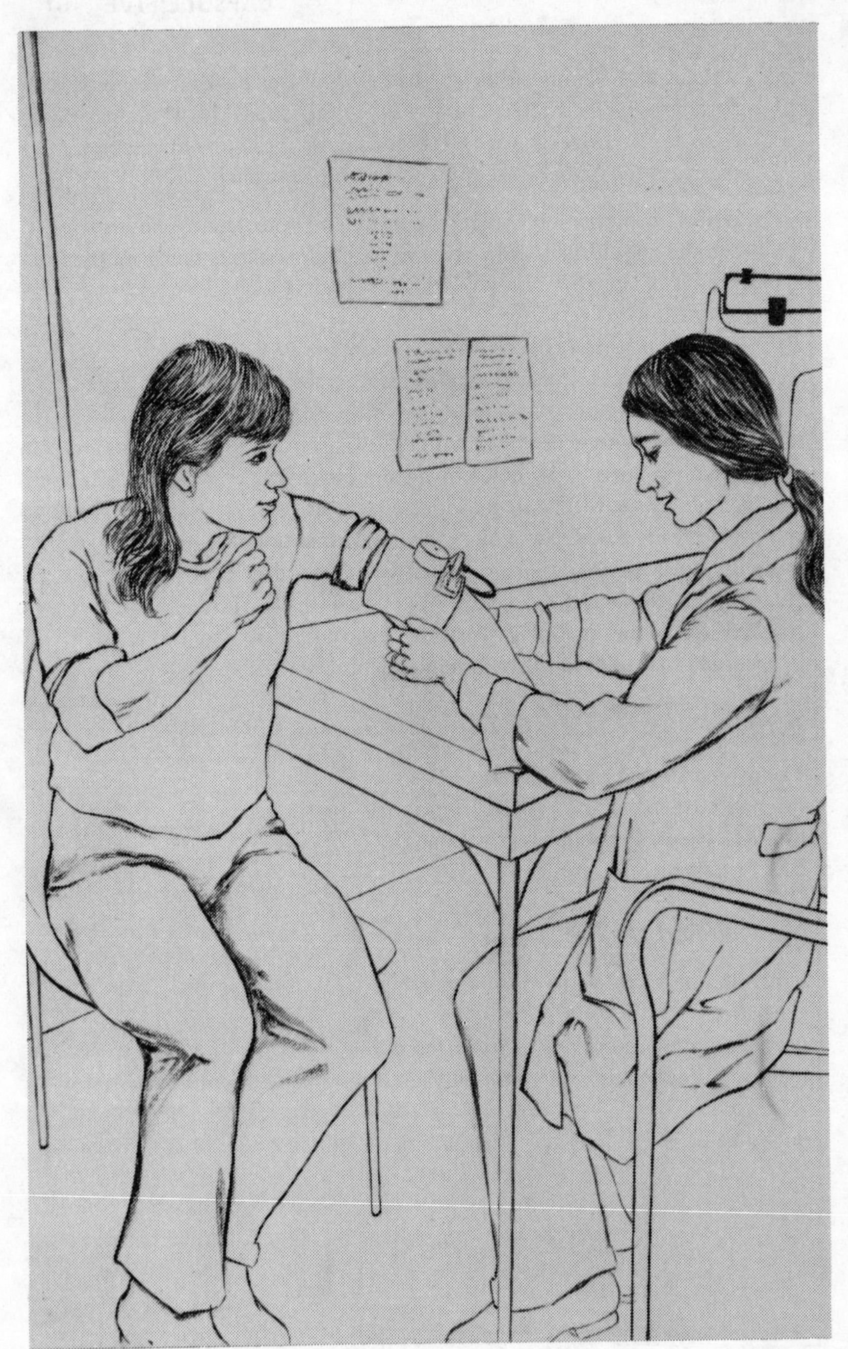

CAPSULE SIX

Staying Fit

DIALOG

Nurse: Good afternoon. May I help you?

Shirley: Yes, I have an appointment to see Dr. Smyth at 3:30.

Nurse: Your name, please?

Shirley: Shirley Copeland.

Nurse: Oh, yes, Ms. Copeland. Come right this way to room number two. Would you please put on this examination gown. The doctor will be with you in one moment.

[Several minutes later.]

Doctor: [a woman] Well, hello, Shirley. Nice to see you again. How are you today?

Shirley: I'm fine, Doctor Smyth, but I felt I should have a checkup before returning to the university. Also, I have to fill out this medical card for the Student Health Service at school.

Doctor: Yes. Well, in any case it's a good idea to have a thorough checkup once a year at least. I think I saw you last year at this time before you left for your freshman year, right?

Shirley: That's right, Doctor, you've got a good memory.

Doctor: Okay. Let's check your height and weight. Umm! It seems that you've gained a few pounds eating that dormitory food. If you continue like that for the next three years, you'll graduate in a size 18!

Shirley: Yes, I was afraid you would notice that. Well, I'm taking swimming this fall quarter, and I hope I can work it off. The truth is, I gained most of this while I was working at Scoops Ice Cream Shop this summer. I'm really not the "junk-food freak" that I once was.

Doctor: Well, I'm glad to hear that. Okay. Let's check your blood pressure. Give me your arm. Umm. Good. Open your mouth and say "Ah."

Shirley: Ahhh!

Doctor: All right. I'm going to look into your ears. Good. Very good. Are your eyes okay? Do you still wear contacts?

Shirley: Yes. In fact I got new contact lenses when I came home for vacation.

Doctor: No problems?

Shirley: Not any more. I'm really used to them.

Doctor: What happened to your eyebrow?

Shirley: I cut it when I fell skiing last winter. That's the scar. The hair is really slow growing in again. Perhaps that's because I scratched the scab.

Doctor: That's natural. Okay, drop the gown to your waist and breathe deeply.

Shirley: Doctor Smyth, when is medicine going to invent a warm stethoscope? They are always so cold.

Doctor: [She chuckles.] Breathe deeply again. Now on your back. Take another deep breath. Still a nonsmoker?

Shirley: Yes.

Doctor: Good. No lumps in your breasts? Fine! Okay. Lie down on the table. I want to check your abdomen. No pain here?

Shirley: No.

Doctor: Here? Do you have frequent stomach pain?

Shirley: No, not really!

Doctor: Excellent. Sit up on the edge of the table, please, and let me test your reflexes. No trouble with that left knee since your ski accident?

Shirley: Not with my knee, Doctor. None. But I feel my ankle is still a little weak. I especially noticed it when I played tennis this spring.

Doctor: Well, you said you'll be swimming this fall term in school; that should help strengthen it. Seems to me that you're fit as a fiddle to start that sophomore year.

Shirley: Doctor Smyth, I think I need some vitamins to give me some strength. I have a busy week ahead of me, and I feel a little run down! Could you suggest something?

Doctor: Too many "end-of-summer" and "back-to-school" parties?

Shirley: Actually, I've left everything to the last minute. As usual, I'm trying to get things ready to go back to school, and I'm doing a week's preparation in three days.

Doctor: That sounds familiar! Okay. I'll write down the names of several good Vitamin B formulas. When you get dressed come into the office, and I'll give them to you.

[Ten minutes later Shirley enters the doctor's office.]

Doctor: Okay. First, let's fill out this University Health Service Card. Let me see, childhood diseases. Measles?

Shirley: Yes.

Doctor: Mumps?

Shirley: No.

Doctor: Chicken pox? Whooping cough?

Shirley: No. Neither of them.

Doctor: That's right. You were a healthy baby. Appendicitis?

Shirley: Never.

Doctor: No dysentery problems?

Shirley: No.

Doctor: You've never been pregnant, correct?

Shirley: Correct.

Doctor: No specific aches or pains? Backache? Stomachache?

Shirley: No. None that I can think of.

Doctor: All right. Your blood pressure is fine. No heart trouble. Looks like you're ready to hit those books once again.

Shirley: Doctor Smyth, do you think you could give me a prescription for some diet pills—just to kill my appetite to try to take off a few pounds. I don't want anything really strong, just something to curb my appetite. Lots of the girls at school were taking them last year. They said they got them from their family doctors.

Doctor: I'm sorry, Shirley, I'd like to help you out but I don't like to prescribe those pills except in extreme cases. I would not consider your case an extreme one, at least not yet! Just a little discipline at mealtime. Don't eat between meals; and maybe go a half hour early to your swimming class. That should take care of those extra five pounds.

Shirley: Okay, Doctor. I guess I was looking for an easy way to do it. Thanks a lot, and I'll see you when I come home in June.

COMPREHENSION QUESTIONS

1. How long has Shirley been seeing Dr. Smyth?
2. How old is Shirley?
3. What is Shirley's major pastime?

PLEASE ANSWER ALL QUESTIONS COMPLETELY AND ACCURATELY IN ORDER TO AVOID DELAYS IN PROCESSING OF THIS APPLICATION.

HEALTH STATEMENT APPLICATION

CHECK COVERAGE YOU WISH TO APPLY FOR:

- ☐ $30 a day Plan
- ☐ Gold Cross
- ☐ Prolonged Illness Plan
- ☐ Family coverage
- ☑ Individual coverage
- ☐ new membership
- ☐ increase membership

Cycle	App.	Eff.	
Cov.	O.E.D.	canc. date	Code

If you are now an active member, please provide your identification number.

IDENTIFICATION # → ____________

1 Applicant's Name (Print) Last ____________ First ____________ Middle ____________
Home Address (Print) Street ____________
City ____________ State ____________ Zip ____________
Check One: ☑ Single ☐ Married ☐ Widowed ☐ Divorced ☐ Legally Separated
SOC. SEC. NO. ____________ Sex ☑ Male ☐ Female
Date of Birth ____________ Height ____________ Weight ____________
Employer's Company Name ____________
Address ____________ ____________

2 Spouse's Name (Print) ____________
Date of Birth ____________
Height ____________ Weight ____________

3 Number of unmarried children under nineteen years of age ____________

4 Have you or any member of your family **to be covered** had any of the following for which you have received treatment in the last three years?

YOU MUST CHECK (✓) EACH PART "YES OR NO". IF "YES" TO ANY, UNDERLINE THE SPECIFIC AILMENTS.

		YES	NO			YES	NO
A	Bronchitis, asthma, tuberculosis	☐	☑	I	Hemorrhoids, rectal ailments.	☐	☑
B	Cysts, tumors, cancer, other growths	☐	☑	J	Gallstones, gall bladder	☐	☑
C	Goiter, thyroid, other throat conditions	☐	☑	K	Kidney stones, kidney	☐	☑
D	High blood pressure, low blood pressure	☐	☑	L	Bladder or prostate condition	☐	☑
E	Eye, ear, nasal conditions	☐	☐	M	Arthritis, bursitis, rheumatism	☐	☑
F	Mental disorders, alcoholism, drug addiction	☐	☐	N	Gynecological conditions	☐	☑
G	Stomach or bowel conditions	☐	☐	O	Hernia, back condition	☐	☑
H	Epilepsy or conditions of nervous system	☐	☐	P	Diabetes	☐	☑

5 Have you or any member of your family **to be covered** had any ailments, injuries, or symptoms of disease in the last three years for which you consulted a physician or psychologist? Yes ☐ No ☑

6 If you have answered "Yes" to questions 4 or 5, indicate the necessary information requested below.

Patient's Name	Treatment and Diagnosis	Date	Physician's Name and Office Address	Hospital Name

7 Do you or any member of your family **to be covered** under this policy need to see a physician or psychologist or need hospital care for any condition that presently exists?

IT IS UNDERSTOOD AND AGREED THAT: (1) I have read the Health Statement Application, understand the questions, and certify that the statements made and answers given are complete and true. (2) Maternity benefits are only allowed after a woman has been covered under a family membership for 8 consecutive months. (3) Coverage for particular diseases or physical conditions may be limited or excluded, etc.

____________ ____________ ____________
Applicant's Signature | Spouse's Signature | Date of Application

STUDENT MEDICAL CARD

Date ______

NAME OF STUDENT (last) ______ (first) ______ (middle) ______

Street Address ______ City ______ State ______ Zip ______

Sex ______ Age ______ Date of Birth ______

DIAGNOSIS

( ) Measles	( ) Scarlet Fever
( ) Mumps	( ) Polio
( ) Chickenpox	( ) Meningitis
( ) German Measles	( ) Tuberculosis
( ) Whooping Cough	( ) Pneumonia
( ) Malaria	( ) Migraine
( ) Encephalitis	( ) Rheumatic Fever
( ) Colitis	( ) Typhoid Fever
( ) Infectious Mononucleosis	( ) Other ______
( ) Anemia	

MEDICAL INSURANCE — If you carry Blue Cross or any other insurance, please list your certificate number and the company's name and address.

4. Why did Shirley go to visit the doctor?
5. How long did Shirley have to wait to see Dr. Smyth?
6. Why had Shirley gained a few extra pounds?
7. How many years has Shirley been studying at the university?
8. How did Shirley get the scar on her eyebrow?
9. Why did Shirley ask for vitamins?
10. What was the doctor's response when Shirley asked for a prescription for diet pills?

VOCABULARY

Words Used in Dialog

abdomen
ache
ankle
appendicitis
appointment
blood pressure
breast
checkup
chicken pox
contacts

diet
dysentery
examination
eyebrows
freshman
gown
heart trouble
height
injection
knee

lumps
measles
mumps
pain
pills
pregnant
prescription
reflex
scab
scar

shot
sophomore
stethoscope
thorough
waist
weak
week
weigh
weight
whooping cough

Phrases

as fit as a fiddle*
between meals
childhood diseases

health service
junk-food freak*
medical card

Verbs

breathe
catch it (in time)*
check
consider
curb (appetite)*
drop
feel run down*

gain
graduate
hit the books*
insist
kill (appetite)*
lose

notice
prescribe
ski
strengthen
take (a class)*
work it off*

VOCABULARY REVIEW

between meals	as fit as a fiddle	prescribe
breathe	health service	scab
catch it in time	hit the books	scar
consider	insist	strengthen
curb (appetite)	junk-food freak	take a class
drop	lose	work (it) off
feel run down	notice	

A. Which of the words or phrases in the Vocabulary Review above could be used meaningfully in the following sentences?

1. As a result of working too hard, she really ________.
2. Many junk-food freaks should ________ in nutrition.
3. Exercise is the best way to ________ excess weight.
4. If you remove a ________ you will probably have a ________.
5. The night before a big test is too late to try to ________.
6. Playing tennis is a good way to ________ your arms and legs.
7. The disease didn't spread because doctors were able to ________.
8. According to this report there is nothing physically wrong with you; in fact, you are ________.
9. In order to lose weight you must ________ your appetite.
10. My mother never allowed us to eat ________; we were allowed to eat only at mealtime.

B. Write an original sentence with each of the following:

1. thorough
   through
   threw
   though
   thought

2. high
   height

3. breathe
   breath

4. weak
   week

5. weigh
   weight
   way

C. Use each group of words and phrases in the given order and form to make an original, meaningful sentence.

Example: people / avoid / diet pills / to lose
People should avoid the use of diet pills to lose weight.

1. vitamins / to avoid / feeling run down
2. between meals / to gain
3. curb (appetite) / healthy / lose
4. diet / affect / health
5. parents / insist / annual checkup

QUESTIONS FOR DISCUSSION

1. Why do you think Shirley worked at Scoops Ice Cream Shop for the summer vacation? Support your answer with information from the dialog. Is it common in your native country for students like Shirley to have such summer jobs? Why or why not?
2. Compare this situation with the last doctor's appointment you had in your native country. What are some similarities and differences?
3. Were you surprised that Dr. Smyth was a woman? Are women doctors common in your native country? Why or why not?
4. How do you think the treatment Shirley got from her "family doctor" was different from the treatment she would have received if she had gone to a clinic? Be specific.

5. Do you know anyone who has ever taken "diet pills"? What effect did you notice in that person? Are these kinds of pills easy to obtain in your native country?

6. What do you know about "socialized" medicine or government-administered health care? Does that type of system operate in your native country? What are some advantages and disadvantages of such systems?

7. Do you think medical service in rural areas of the United States differs greatly from health service and care in the urban areas? If so, why? In your native country is there a difference in the health service in the urban and in the rural areas?

SUGGESTED ACTIVITIES

1. Collect current English language magazine and newspaper articles which discuss new trends in modern medical practice. For example, explore new thinking with regard to natural child birth, acupuncture, or organ transplants. Report to the class.

2. With another member of the class prepare a short mini-drama enacting a discussion in a doctor's waiting room between a person who is obviously nervous on this, his first visit to the doctor, and a hypochondriac. The hypochondriac obviously wants to discuss all his past illnesses, and the other patient obviously does not want to hear about them.

3. List some of the health and medical problems in your native country. After discussing them with other students, write a composition explaining them and suggesting some ways to solve the problems, if you can.

4. Investigate modern medical findings with regard to "diet pills" or amphetamines. What are the dangers of these kinds of pills? Why do people take them? Report to the class.

5. If you are in the United States, contact Weight Watchers or a similar organization and obtain information and literature from them. Report to the class.

6. Write a composition or tell the class about an interesting part-time job which you once had (or now have). Why did you take the job? What interesting experiences did you have as a result of the job?

7. Do you have any medical insurance coverage? What kind of coverage does your policy offer? Bring your policy to class, and as a group discuss the different benefits that are included. Be sure you know how to fill out the sample claim form that is included in this capsule.

GLOSSARY

Phrases

as fit as a fiddle—in excellent health.
junk-food freak—slang for a person who eats all kinds of food which has little nutritional value.

Verbs

catch it (in time)—realize a potential problem and control it before it becomes a serious difficulty.
curb (appetite)—control one's desire to eat.
feel run down—feel exhausted.
hit the books—study hard.
kill (appetite)—eliminate the desire to eat.
take (a class)—enroll in.
work it off—in this case to lose weight by doing physical exercise.

VOCABULARY REVIEW, CAPSULES 4 to 6

assistantship
to bloom
coming right up
to complicate
creature of comfort
experience is the best teacher
extract
as fit as a fiddle
to live off
in a jiffy
in a pinch
junk-food freak
novelty has worn off

prescription
to recommend
right you are
(to be) run down
to settle for
to stock up on
to take (you) up on (something)
to take the edge off
vegetarian
wasting (your) life away
to wonder
to work off
would you believe

Which of the words or phrases listed above could be used meaningfully in the following sentences? It may be necessary to make changes in the forms of the words.

1. A person who eats no meat or dairy products is a strict ____________.
2. When something which was once new and exciting becomes commonplace and routine, you might say that it's ____________.
3. To buy in advance, keeping on hand a supply of necessary items, is to ____________ certain staples.
4. If you accept someone's offer, you ____________ them ____________ it.
5. Count on Ted to help you out ____________.
6. Someone who does not feel productive in his life or career might feel that he is ____________.
7. If you make a situation more difficult, then you have ____________ the situation.
8. To exist on the earnings of another person is to ____________ him.
9. If the food is just about ready to be served, you might say it's ____________.
10. To reduce the effect of something is ____________.
11. A person who loves to eat popcorn, candy, soda pop, doughnuts, cake, and cookies might be considered a ____________.
12. A man might be 89 years old, but his body can still be ____________.
13. If you have no energy and feel tired and listless, maybe you are just ____________.
14. Medications that might be harmful require a doctor's ____________.
15. Exercise is the best way ____________ unwanted weight.

CAPSULE SEVEN

The Blacker the Berry

DIALOG

Genie: Well, you're back late. I was worried. How's the car? What did you find out?

Bob: Maybe you'd better sit down before I break the news to you.

Genie: Oh! Don't be such a tease! Did you pick up the car?

Bob: Tease! I wish I were teasing. I'm dead serious. The mechanic said that the best thing would be to trade it in and get a new car. This car is a total loss.

Genie: Oh, Bob! You're kidding. You must be kidding! Not really?!!

Bob: Yes, really. Genie, do I look like I'm joking? Heaven knows, I wish it were just a bad dream! The mechanic said it would take at least ten days to fix it up and it would cost a lot. And even then he couldn't guarantee how much longer it would last.

Genie: Do you trust the mechanic? Maybe he saw your black face and figured he could take you for a ride.

Bob: Look, Genie. You've got to get over this idea you have of mistrusting every white person with whom you come in contact. You're in the North now, Baby. Things aren't perfect up here, but you've got to give people a chance.

Genie: Oh! So prejudice is only a reality in Dixie, is that what you're saying?

Bob: Let's not have this same discussion again. We'll just end up going in circles. Our problem of the moment is not the social injustices of the world. Our problem is what to do about the car.

Genie: I'm sorry, Honey, but I find your total acceptance of the white man in his white-controlled world a bit difficult to understand and even more difficult to accept. I know the South is no utopia, but sometimes I . . .

Bob: . . . I know, sometimes you just wish you could smell magnolia blossoms and drink mint juleps. Baby, your memory seems awfully short. Have you forgotten those letters you used to write from Fisk when you and all the other university students would have sit-ins at the local restaurants? You weren't so big on the South then.

Genie: Here we go again. Back to the same old discussion. Forget it, I'm sorry I even mentioned it. Let's try to solve our own immediate problem. What else did the mechanic tell you? Exactly what is wrong with the car? Can it be driven?

Bob: No, it shouldn't be driven. According to the mechanic, the cylinder block is cracked and one of the piston rings is broken.

Genie: Would that account for the knocking sound I hear?

Bob: It most certainly would!

Genie: How much trade-in do you think we can get for it in this condition?

Bob: On my way home I stopped at the showroom on Clark Street. That's why I'm late. Without seeing the car they can't tell me exactly what they'd give for a trade-in. But they checked and the blue book lists that model and that year at $850, top trade-in.

Genie: Oh, Bob! I don't want to start paying car notes again. It seems we just finished paying off this car. And I was hoping we could get a new refrigerator. I've got it! Maybe we should take the old car to another mechanic, just to see what he says. Maybe he could somehow patch it up.

Bob: Genie, another mechanic will just tell us the same thing. If he's honest he'll say the car is shot, and he'll be right. Let's face it and start looking for a new car.

Genie: Hey! Why don't we buy a good used car? That way we wouldn't have to go into debt so heavily for a car. And maybe we could still buy that new refrigerator.

Bob: Look, Genie, when you buy a used car you're just buying someone else's problems. Used-car dealers just try to cover up mechanical defects with a new coat of paint and new set of tires. No one gets rid of a car that is giving good service.

Genie: That makes sense.

Bob: There was a really good-looking sedan displayed in the Clark Street showroom. Do you want to go take a look at it?

Genie: Well, we might as well start facing reality now. Let me run a comb through my hair and I'll be ready.

[Several hours later Genie and Bob enter the showroom of the automobile center on Clark Street.]

Salesman: So, you're back, Mr. Harris. Good afternoon, Mrs. Harris. All the models we have are here on display in the showroom, although there are several different colors in the back lot.

Genie: Oh, look Bob! This is sure a good-looking car, isn't it?

Salesman: Yes, that's a handsome automobile, Mrs. Harris. You certainly have good taste. This is our deluxe four-door sedan.

Genie: I'd like to know what other colors it comes in.

Bob: Colors! Oh, Genie! What I'd like to know is, how many miles does it get to the gallon?

Salesman: Well, uh, I'm not certain, but this car has air conditioning, power brakes, push-button windows . . .

Bob: And how much does this car cost?

Salesman: $6,700, without extras, of course. We can offer you a generous trade-in on your old car, and you can arrange for our easy-payment plan.

Bob: Maybe we'd better look at less expensive models.

Salesman: Our compact model is very popular this year.

Genie: Oh, I love this color. And look, Bob, there's a hole in the roof.

Bob: Right! It's the compact's economy answer to air conditioning!

Salesman: That's our sun-roof model. Basically it's the same as the standard compact, with the addition of the open roof and the deluxe seats.

Genie: The seats *are* nice. Are they leather?

Salesman: Well, not exactly. They're vinyl, but they are very durable and have a twelve-month guarantee against defects.

Bob: [Aside to Genie.] And you're the one who's always worried about tanning yourself so dark. Now you want to drive around the city with a hole in the roof of your car with the sun beating down on you. Ah! Women! I'll just never understand them.

Genie: When did I ever say that I didn't want . . .

Bob: Look, Baby. It won't bother me how dark you get. You know what they say, "The blacker the berry the sweeter the juice." [He laughs.]

Genie: Oh, go on!

COMPREHENSION QUESTIONS

1. Why was Bob late coming home from seeing the mechanic?
2. What did the mechanic say was wrong with the car?
3. Why did Genie suggest going to see another mechanic?
4. What part of the United States is Genie from?
5. Did Genie go to college? If so, where?
6. How do Genie and Bob feel about white people?
7. What was Bob's feeling about buying a used car?
8. How did the salesman try to make it easy for them to purchase a car?
9. Describe the two cars they looked at.
10. What seemed to be important to Genie when thinking about buying a new car? To Bob?

VOCABULARY

Words Used in Dialog

blue-book price*
compact
cylinder block
defects
durable
Fisk*
generous
good-looking
guarantee
piston rings
prejudice
racial
sedan
shot
showroom
sun roof*
trade-in
utopia
vinyl

Phrases

a total loss
break the news*
car note
coat of paint
easy-payment plan
going in circles*
knocking sound
less expensive
magnolia*
mint julep*
on display
peaches and cream*
sit-in*
top trade-in*

Verbs

account for*
arrange
get rid of
go heavily into debt
patch it up*
pay off*

bother	guarantee	take a look at
cover up	kid	tease
find out	mistrust	trade in
fix it up		

Slang

Baby*	go on*	take for a ride*
Dixie	Honey*	

VOCABULARY REVIEW

a total loss	find out	mistrust
arrange	generous	offer
break the news	guarantee	pay off
car note	injustice	patch it up
coats (of paint)	(to) kid	take you for a ride
durable	less expensive	take a look
easy-payment plan	mechanic	top trade-in

A. Rewrite the following sentences using words or phrases in the Vocabulary Review above to replace the italicized portions.

1. I want to try to *schedule* a visit to the museum for their visit.
2. Shopping at that store is *much cheaper* than going downtown.
3. Basically, I just *don't have any confidence in* him.
4. The accident left the car *without any value whatsoever.*
5. When I painted the desk I had to put several *different layers* of paint on it.
6. Some people always like to be the first to *tell what happened.*
7. Why don't we go to the shopping center just to *see what they have.*
8. If you aren't careful, door-to-door salesmen can *make a fool out of you.*
9. My older brother always used to *tease* me about my freckles.
10. If she buys a new car, the *most she can possibly get* for her old car is $150.

B. Use each group of words and phrases in the given order and form to make an original, meaningful sentence.

Example: supermarket / to beat the crowd
I went to the supermarket early to beat the crowd.

1. reluctant / go into debt / car note
2. mechanic / patch it up / coat of paint
3. take a look at / compact / display room
4. break the news / car / total loss
5. account for / noise

C. Read the following short paragraph. When you have finished reading, close your book and then try to rewrite the paragraph from memory. The instructor will have a list of guide words on the blackboard to help you.

Some people prefer to buy a used car instead of buying a new car. One reason is that older cars were often built better, with more resistance, than today's cars. Another reason is that the cost of a used car is much less than the cost of a new car. However, buying a used car is often buying someone else's problems. Unless you are mechanically inclined and are able to make minor repairs on your "new used car," you often find that the first trip you take is to visit the mechanic at the nearest garage.

QUESTIONS FOR DISCUSSION

1. Using information from the dialog, what can you say about Genie and Bob's education, income, racial attitudes, sense of humor, and attitudes about money? Explain in detail.
2. What are the advantages of fixing up an old car as opposed to buying a new car? What would you do in that situation? Why?
3. What are the advantages and disadvantages of buying on the "easy-payment" plan? Does your native country offer such buying plans? How are they different from those plans in the United States?

4. When buying a new car, what are the important things you should look for? What are the advantages and disadvantages of a full-sized car as compared with a compact car?

5. What do you think of Genie's immediate mistrust of the white mechanic? Why do you think she reacted in this manner?

6. Are there any racial prejudices in your native country? If so, explain them. If not, why do you think they don't exist?

7. What do you think the expression, "The blacker the berry the sweeter the juice" means? Why do you think Bob said it at that particular moment? Can you think of a modern version of the same saying?

SUGGESTED ACTIVITIES

1. Consult *Consumer Report, Motor Trend,* or other United States periodicals which report on the new models of cars. Prepare a report for the class on which new-model car you think is the best buy for this year.

2. Have you ever purchased a car? Write a composition describing the circumstances of this purchase.

3. With other members of the class, prepare a mini-drama in which you enact the scene of a well-dressed man (woman) who comes into the display room to look at the new cars. The salesman doesn't know that the customer has little money, and so he tries desperately to sell him an expensive new car.

4. Write a composition in which you attempt to persuade your reader about one of the following:
   - A compact is better than a full-sized car.
   - A full-sized car is better than a compact.
   - A used car is better than a new car.
   - A new car is better than a used car.

5. Have you personally ever been a victim of racial or religious prejudice? If so, share this experience with the class.

6. Consult the *Reader's Guide to Periodical Literature* in the library for articles in United States publications from the middle 1960s which relate the many sit-ins and demonstrations that occurred in

the South during that time. *Ebony Magazine* and the *Negro Digest* (now changed to *Black Truth*) are publications which may be interesting to read. Prepare an oral or written report.

7. If you are interested in reading about the situation of black people in the United States in the 1930s and 1940s, you may want to read the short stories of Richard Wright, a famous black author of this time. *Uncle Tom's Children* is a collection of five short stories, all of which give a vivid account of this period in United States history.

GLOSSARY

Vocabulary

blue-book price—refers to a list published by car dealers which states the highest and lowest possible prices for a used car of a specific model.
Fisk—a well-known, highly respected university in the South which used to be only for black students.
sun roof—a car model which has an opening in the roof to allow sun and air to enter directly. It is not completely open, as in a convertible.

Phrases

break the news—tell someone news (usually bad).
going in circles—being busy but not accomplishing anything.
magnolia—a tree, typical to parts of the southern United States, which produces large, fragrant flowers.
mint julep—an alcoholic drink that is popular in parts of the southern United States.
peaches and cream—fine, beautiful, without problems.
sit-ins—demonstrations prevalent in the 1960s when students would sit down in a restaurant or other location to protest discrimination against blacks; a nonviolent demonstration of social protest.
top trade-in—the highest value listed in the automobile blue book.

Verbs

account for—explain the reason that something happened.
patch it up—fix it up.
pay off—to finish paying for something that was purchased on time payments.

Nonstandard English

Baby; Honey—affectionate terms used between men and women.
go on—literally it means go away; in this sense it means to quit joking and straighten up.
take for a ride—exploit a person; to take advantage of their ignorance.

PIES
CAKES

CAPSULE EIGHT

Blue-Collar Blues

DIALOG

[Rural Midwest accent]

Waitress: Yeah, what'll it be?

Willard: Cup of coffee, Honey.

Waitress: Here you are. Anything else?

Willard: I'll have a chocolate-covered doughnut, too.

Waitress: Right!

Hank: Good morning, Willard. What brings you out to breakfast in such a fancy place as this? Your ol' lady put you out of the house? Or you just like this truck stop?

Willard: You hit the nail on the head! I had to get out of my house or go crazy. The kids are off to school by 8:15, and Sara's doing the dishes and the housework. I just sit around; you can read the want ads just so long, and then they begin to blur.

Hank: Yeah, I sure understand that. Hey, Sweetheart!

Waitress: What's yours?

Hank: A cup of coffee and an order of French toast.

Waitress: Sure thing. Here's your coffee. French toast coming right up.

Hank: How long since you were laid off?

Willard: Going on three and a half months.

Hank: Haven't been able to find nothin', huh?

Willard: I've filled out so many job applications I've lost count. Always the same old story, "Thank you very much, Mr. Moore. Don't call us, we'll call you."

Hank: Yeah! Ain't easy.

Willard: Let's face it. Nobody wants to hire a thirty-seven-year-old man with a wife and three kids to support. If you don't mind me asking, how've you managed?

Hank: Ain't been easy. It got so bad at one point that we had to get rid of the dogs. Just about broke my son's heart, but we couldn't hardly put food on the table for us, and two full-grown German Shepherds eat a lot. Yeah, it got really bad there for a while, when my unemployment ran out and no hope of a job. Can you believe those guys? A man gives twenty-one years to the same company, and one day they just come up and say, "So long, Charley."

Waitress: Here's your French toast. More coffee?

Hank: Yeah. Fine.

Willard: Me, too. Got more cream?

Waitress: Here you go.

Willard: Thanks. Yeah, I'd been at this plant for seventeen and a half years. It's the only job I really know. If I don't find something pretty soon, I don't know what'll happen.

Hank: What about Sara? If Mabel hadn't started working as a checker at the supermarket, we'd all be starving.

Willard: Well, we talked about her going to work. Little Willy is in school now; he's the youngest. But Sara isn't trained to do anything. She never worked a day in her life.

Hank: Mabel was in the same boat. But our kids are all in school too. She ain't got nothing to keep her at home. When she started working, we agreed it would only be till I landed a job. Then she really got to liking it. Every night she comes home full of the supermarket gossip. When I got the nightwatchman job at the bank, she decided to stay on at the supermarket. Sure, the extra money comes in handy, but it ain't like before, when she had to work or else.

Willard: How do you feel about her working? I mean, don't it bother you?

Hank: Well, Will, at first I couldn't stand the thought of my ol' lady out there working and me at home, reading the want ads. You know, it's hard on a guy. I don't give a damn what these crazy Women's Liberation people say, I was brought up to believe "A woman's place is in the home."

Willard: That's what I was brought up to believe too. But then, on the farm, there's not much chance for a woman to go about looking for a job. Sara and I both come from the farm. We moved here to Libertyville the year we were married. I worked at the gas station, till I got on at the plant. Would seem mighty strange, Sara going off to work in the morning.

Waitress: Fill it up?

Hank: Yep, go ahead.

Willard: Thanks.

Hank: Well, it ain't easy. But it'll take the pressure off you a while. That way you can look for a job without all the worry of what your family's gonna eat.

Willard: Maybe I should go home and talk with Sara.

Hank: Say, Mabel mentioned there's an opening coming up at the supermarket. Seems Janet Green's gonna have her baby soon. Might be Sara could get on there. They give 10 percent discount to exployees. Ain't a lot, but with all the food we pack away, it adds up.

Willard: Thanks, Hank. I appreciate your efforts. Can we have the checks, Honey?

Waitress: Here you are. One coffee and a doughnut . . . 45 cents.

Willard: There you go.

Waitress: Thanks. And let's see, coffee and a French toast, $1.05.

Hank: Here you go. Keep the change, Sweetheart.

Waitress: Thanks. Have a nice day.

COMPREHENSION QUESTIONS

1. Why was Willard at the Truck Stop Café so early in the morning?
2. Why was Willard looking for a new job?
3. What seems to have been Willard's feeling in the past about working wives?
4. What is Hank's philosophy about working wives?
5. What are some advantages for Hank's family, as a result of his wife's working in the supermarket?
6. How does Mabel feel about her job?
7. What is Hank's current job?
8. Why hasn't Willard's wife gone to look for a job?
9. Where did Willard and Sara grow up? When did they move away?
10. Describe Hank and Willard in terms of education and income.

VOCABULARY

Words Used in Dialog

blue-collar*	compensation	ego
checker*	discount	employees

CL.	CD.	OFF. NO.	EFF. WK.	ITIN. CD.	DEPEND	MALE ☐	FEMALE ☐
SERVICE SERIAL NO.					CLM TAKER	REG. ☐	X-C ☐
TO PROCESS					PS ☐	FE ☐	UCX ☐

LO	OTHER	OCCUPATION	
		IP	WR
LO	OTHER		
		IP	WR
LO	OTHER		
		IP	WR
LO	OTHER		
		IP	WR

OBY — YES ☐ NO ☐

ALL REQUIRED NOTICES MAILED (Except as noted above)

CN.............By ....Clk.

SINGLE ☐ MULTIPLE ☐

CLAIM FOR BENEFITS (Complete all items below)

(Social Security Account Number)

1. NAME AND SOC. SEC. ACCT. NO. ....
   (First Name) (Middle Initial) (Last Name)
2. MAIL ADDRESS ....
   (No. and Street, P. O. Box or RFD No.) (City or Town) (Zip Code)
3. DATE OF BIRTH
4. *STATEMENT: I hereby state under the penalties of perjury that: I am currently unemployed because of* (1) ☐ LACK OF WORK (2) ☐ QUIT (3) ☐ DISCHARGE (4) ☐ LABOR DISPUTE; *I understand that each time I sign my Claim Record Card that all statements entered thereon are true and correct to the best of my knowledge and belief; I have received Form 2594 setting forth the conditions specified by law which I must comply with in order to qualify for benefits. I hereby register for work and claim benefits.*

   READ CAREFULLY BEFORE SIGNING

   Date of Filing ________ Signature of Claimant ____________________
5. LIST ALL OF THE JOBS AT WHICH YOU HAVE WORKED SINCE

			DATE STARTED	DATE SEPARATED
MOST RECENT JOB	NAME OF FIRM (not foreman or owner)			
	STREET ADDRESS		CITY OR TOWN	
	OCCUPATION	OTHER NAMES OR SSA NOS. USED (if any)	DO NOT WRITE HERE	
SECOND MOST RECENT JOB	NAME OF FIRM (not foreman or owner)		DATE STARTED	DATE SEPARATED
	STREET ADDRESS		CITY OR TOWN	
	OCCUPATION	OTHER NAMES OR SSA NOS. USED (if any)		

6. DO YOU HAVE DEPENDENT CHILDREN UNDER THE AGE OF EIGHTEEN? .... YES ☐ NO ☐
7. DO YOU HAVE PHYSICALLY OR MENTALLY INCAPACITATED CHILDREN OF ANY AGE? .... YES ☐ NO ☐
8. DO YOU HAVE ANY DEPENDENTS OVER THE AGE OF 18 WHO ARE STUDENTS ATTENDING SCHOOL ON A FULL-TIME BASIS? .... YES ☐ NO ☐
9. ARE THERE ANY PERSONAL, DOMESTIC, OR OTHER REASONS WHICH WOULD PREVENT YOU FROM ACCEPTING WORK ON ANY FULL TIME SHIFT WHICH IS CUSTOMARY TO YOUR OCCUPATION? .... YES ☐ NO ☐
10. ARE YOU ON A LEAVE OF ABSENCE FROM YOUR EMPLOYER? .... YES ☐ NO ☐
11. ARE YOU RECEIVING, HAVE YOU RECEIVED, OR DO YOU EXPECT TO RECEIVE SEPARATION OR DISMISSAL PAY, VACATION ALLOWANCES OR WORKMEN'S COMPENSATION OR A RETIREMENT BENEFIT? .... YES ☐ NO ☐
12. ARE OR WERE ANY OF THE BUSINESSES YOU HAVE LISTED AS HAVING WORKED FOR OWNED OR PARTLY OWNED BY YOURSELF OR BY YOUR SON, DAUGHTER, SPOUSE, FATHER OR MOTHER? .... YES ☐ NO ☐
13. ARE YOU PRESENTLY ENGAGED IN ANY BUSINESS ACTIVITY EITHER AS AN INDIVIDUAL, PARTNER OR MEMBER OF A CORPORATION? .... YES ☐ NO ☐
14. HAVE YOU FILED A CLAIM AT THIS OR AT ANY OTHER EMPLOYMENT OFFICE DURING THE PAST 12 MONTHS? .... YES ☐ NO ☐

PENSION	
YES ☐	NO ☐
AMOUNT Per Month	
AMOUNT Per Week	

gas station
gossip
nightwatchman
plant*
truck stop*
unemployment
want ads

Phrases

at one point
can't stand (the thought of)
comes in handy*
coming right up
going on (time)*
have a nice day
here you are/go*
if you don't mind
in the same boat*
off to school
or else
there you are/go*

Verbs

blur
break one's heart
bring up (to believe)
face it*
get rid of*
hit the nail on the head*
lay off*
put out (of the house)
keep the change
starve
stay on*
support

Slang

ain't
damn
get on*
land (a job)*
mighty*
ol' lady*
pack away*
run out of . . .*
a sure thing
yeah

VOCABULARY REVIEW

a sure thing
at one point
be brought up
blur
can't stand
comes in handy
discount
get rid of
going on (time)
if you don't mind
in the same boat
keep the change
be laid off
off to school
pack away
stay on
support

A. Rewrite the following sentences, replacing the italicized portion with a word or phrase from the Vocabulary Review above.

1. He's been without work ever since he *was asked to leave* the job.
2. My grandparents *were trained* to believe that "Children should be seen and not heard."
3. Remember when you broke your arm? Well, I'm *in the same situation* now!

4. *If it doesn't bother you*, may I turn on the television?

5. I've resigned my job as of August, but they asked if I would *keep on working* until they hire someone else.

6. My grandfather always said I could *keep whatever money was left over* after I went to the store to buy his chocolates.

7. When our cat kept trying to eat the fish, we had to *give* them *away*.

8. That man certainly can *eat a lot of* pancakes!

9. The new job isn't *certain*; I'll know definitely on Friday.

10. He just *can't accept* the idea that a lady is going to drive a taxi.

B. Which of the words listed above in the Vocabulary Review could be used meaningfully in the following sentences?

1. My uncle only bets on ______________.

2. I watched so much television my eyes began to ______________.

3. I'd like to borrow a cigarette ______________.

4. ______________ during my university studies, I wanted to quit and go to work to make money. But I'm glad I didn't, now.

5. It's difficult to ______________ a family when you don't have a steady income.

C. Rewrite the following sentences from the dialog in standard English.

1. Haven't been able to find nothin', huh?

2. Ain't easy.

3. Ain't been easy.

4. Just about broke my son's heart, but we couldn't hardly put food on the table for us.

5. Got more cream?

6. She ain't got nothin' to keep her at home.

7. It ain't like before.

8. Don't it bother you?

9. Would seem mighty strange.
10. Seems Janet Green's gonna have her baby soon.
11. Might be Sara could get on there.
12. Ain't a lot, but with all the food we pack away, it adds up.

QUESTIONS FOR DISCUSSION

1. Why is Willard having such a difficult time finding a job? Explain.
2. What is the difference between a "blue-collar" worker and a "white-collar" worker? In which of those categories would you place Willard? Hank?
3. Is unemployment a problem in your native country? What compensation does your government make? Compare how this situation is handled in the United States and in your native country.
4. How do you think Mabel and Sara feel about their situations? Explain your answer.
5. Describe the communication between the two men and the waitress. Is this typical of a similar conversation in your native country? What differences did you see?
6. Compare the speech of Hank and Willard to characters in the other dialogs you have read. Are there similar speech differences in your native country? Explain, and give some examples.
7. How do you feel about working wives? Do you think it makes a difference if the husband isn't working? Do you think it makes a difference if the husband is working but isn't earning very much money? What if the wife wants to work for her own personal satisfaction? Is the "working wife" typical in your native country? What were Hank and Willard's reactions to the idea of a working wife?
8. Write a short composition in which you describe a difficult experience you had trying to get a passport, visa, scholarship, or admission to school. What were the reactions of the officials you had to talk to? What were your feelings? How did you react? Did you reveal your true feelings? Why or why not?

9. What is the meaning of the expression "Children should be seen and not heard"? Do you agree? Why or why not? Is there a similar expression in your native country?

SUGGESTED ACTIVITIES

1. With another member of the class, prepare a mini-drama in which you create a conversation between Mabel and Sara discussing their current situations, and the possiblity of Sara's going to work.
2. Write a composition or give a speech in class, in which you state your ideas concerning the working wife.
3. If you are living in the United States, find out the procedure for applying for and obtaining unemployment benefits or compensation. Who is eligible and under what conditions? Report to the class.
4. If you are living in the United States, investigate the employment agencies that exist in your communities. What is the procedure for someone applying for a job? Does the agency charge a fee? What kinds of jobs do they advertise? Report to the class.
5. Have you ever been desperate to locate a job? If so, share this experience with the class in oral or written form.

GLOSSARY

Vocabulary

blue-collar—pertaining to people who work with their hands.
checker—a clerk who totals up the cost of purchases in a supermarket and takes the money.
plant—factory.
truck stop—a roadside restaurant where truck drivers stop to eat.

Phrases

comes in handy—is convenient or useful.
going on (time)—almost (8:00).
here/there you are/go—this is for you.
in the same boat—in the same situation.

Verbs

face it—accept it.
get rid of—destroy or eliminate.
hit the nail on the head—be exactly right.
lay off—fire.
stay on—continue doing the same as before.

Nonstandard English

get on—be hired.
land (**a job**)—get.
mighty—very.
ol' lady—wife (see capsule 1).
pack away—eat a lot.
run out of—use up; have no more.

ECI

THE ENGINEERING CO., INC.
APPLICATION FOR EMPLOYMENT

Date: ______________ Social Security No. ______________ Phone No. ____________

Name: ____
Last First Middle

Address: ____
Street City Zip Code

Single ☐ Married ☐ Separated ☐ Divorced ☐ Widowed ☐

U.S. Citizen: Yes ☐ No ☐ Height ____________ Weight ____________

Number of children ________

List other dependents: ____

Previously employed by this firm? ________ Which department? ______________

List all serious operations, accidents, illnesses, disabilities and limitations. (If none, so state):

____

Have you ever received Workmen's Compensation for an industrial injury/illness? (Describe):

____

Have you ever been convicted of a criminal offense (other than parking and minor traffic citations)? If Yes, explain: ____

EDUCATION (Give school, location, years attended, area of concentration)

High School: ____

College: ____

Trade or business school: ____

U.S. Military Service? (Branch and years of service): ______________________

Are you now in any military organization? ______________________________

Previous employment (list last job first)

From: ______________________ To: ______________________

Employer: ____

Salary: ______________________ Position: ______________________

Reason for leaving: ____

From: ______________________ To: ______________________

Employer: ____

Salary: ______________________ Position: ______________________

Reason for leaving: ______________________________________

CHECK BELOW THE MACHINES THAT YOU HAVE OPERATED OR SKILLS YOU HAVE:

☐ Bridgeport	☐ Planer	☐ Blueprinting Machine
☐ Miller, Vertical	☐ Vertical Shaper	☐ Teletype
☐ Miller, Tracing	☐ Blanchard Grinder	☐ Posting Machine
☐ Mill, Horizontal Boring	☐ Surface Grinder	☐ Adding Machine
☐ Screw Cutter	☐ Cylindrical Grinder	☐ Calculator
(Type)	☐ N/C Machinery	☐ Keypunch
☐ Dye Mill	(Type)	☐ Key Sort
☐ Turret Lathe	☐ Typewriter _______WPM	☐ Tabulator
(Type)	☐ Shorthand _______WPM	☐ PBX
☐ EDM Machine	☐ Speedwriting _____ WPM	☐ Lift Trucks
☐ Engine Lathe	☐ Bookkeeping Machine	☐ Welding Machine
☐ Radial Drill		☐ Hand Tools

References: PLEASE LIST THE NAME OF THREE PERSONS, NOT RELATED TO YOU, WHO YOU HAVE KNOWN FOR AT LEAST ONE YEAR

____

____

____

I certify that the statements I have made in this application are true and I authorize The Engineering Co., Inc. to investigate the accuracy and completeness of this information.

It is understood that as a prerequisite to consideration for employment by The Engineering Co., Inc. I agree to submit to such future examination, physical or other, as may be required.

In the event of employment, I expressly understand that any false or misleading statements made by me in this application or in connection with my physical examination will be sufficient grounds for immediate dismissal from employment.

____

Signature of applicant

For office use:

Hired _________ For Dept. _________ Position _________ Will Report _________

Wages _________ Approval ______________________ Date _________

CAPSULE NINE

Apartment Hunting

DIALOG

[A doorbell rings.]

Bill: Coming! I'm coming!

[He opens the door.]

Morning, Steve. Wow! What'd you do, buy out the newspaper stand on the corner?

Steve: Well, I thought we might as well have a copy of each paper in order to have a good selection of want ads.

Bill: Good idea. Come on into the kitchen. Do you want some coffee? We might as well look for an apartment in comfort.

Steve: Coffee sounds good. Here, you take *The Sun* and *The Gazette.* I'll take *The News* and *The Tribune.* Circle anything that looks promising.

Bill: Did we decide on a top rent figure?

Steve: Well, I can't go any higher than $125 a month, and I'd like to keep it under $100.

Bill: Hey, Man! Just what do you plan to do with the rest of your salary? Are you planning on saving your first million before you reach thirty? If I had your job I'd be renting the penthouse of some new, fancy high-rise, complete with sun deck, pool, saunas, and tennis courts. Before I forget—congratulations on your new promotion.

Steve: Thanks. Hey! How'd you find out? It's supposed to be a big, dark company secret until the end of the month.

Bill: Your mother told my mother at some meeting last week.

Steve: I should have guessed. The proud parent couldn't keep a secret. Unfortunately, that raise is spent even before I have it. I've got to begin to pay back my college loan, now that I've been out more than a year. And my parents loaned me the down payment for my car. I want to get those debts off my back and I want to save some money to travel. Next year I plan to take off and do South America.

Bill: Okay, $200 to $225 top rent. Two bedrooms. Do we want furnished or unfurnished?

Steve: What do you think?

Bill: Furnished is easier and in the long run it's cheaper. But if we find a two-bedroom, unfurnished, bachelor paradise—you know, fireplace, panoramic view, balcony, etc.—we can always furnish it cheaply with a couple of waterbeds and beanbag chairs.

Steve: Right! And my mother said I could take anything I want from the old furniture she has stored in the basement. We can take a look at it later on. Hey! Where are your parents and sisters? Sure seems quiet here.

Bill: They're at the lake for Labor Day weekend. They'll come back on Tuesday; that's why I'd like to find a place today or tomorrow, so I can get moved in before they all come back. It'll just be easier—fewer people and less commotion.

Steve: Good idea. Do you know how Rich and Gerry found their place? They just decided which neighborhood they wanted to live in and they walked up and down the streets reading the "For Rent" signs posted on the doors. Those signs give all the information; how much rent, how many rooms, when available, and who to contact.

Bill: Not a bad idea. But why don't we take a fast look through the want ads to see if anything catches our eye? More coffee? Or do you want a cold beer?

Steve: One cup of coffee a day is my limit. Better give me a beer. I don't have any limit on beers. Hey! How does this sound? Four rooms; two bedrooms; living-dining combination; parquet floors; fireplace; immediate occupancy.

Bill: Sounds terrific! Doesn't say how much. It's listed under central location. Shall I call? There's a number listed.

Steve: Right. You call, I'll keep on looking through the paper.

[There is the sound of a phone being dialed.]

Bill: Hello. I'm calling about the ad in this morning's *Sun*, regarding a four-room apartment for rent. Is it still available? _______________ It is? Great! Pardon me, but how much are you asking for the rent? _______________ Four hundred dollars!!?? Thank you, I'm afraid that's a bit more than we had planned to spend. Good-bye.

Steve: Four hundred dollars! That's $100 per room. Did you ask where it was?

Bill: I forgot such details. The rent left me speechless. The place must have been completely furnished, including ten years' free supply of firewood for the fireplace. Have you run across anything else in the newspaper?

Steve: Here's one that looks promising. Two-bedroom apartment. Sunny with view of city. Perfect for students. Reasonable rent. Available immediately. You're a medical student, so we at least qualify on that score. You want to call?

Bill: Okay. What's the number?

Steve: 684-8457.

[The sound of a phone being dialed.]

Bill: Hello. I'm calling about the apartment you have listed in this morning's paper. ______________ Ah! It is. Well, thank you.

Steve: Rented?

Bill: Rented!

Steve: As long as you're by the phone, try calling this one. It says, two large bedrooms; living-dining combination; unfurnished; fireplace; reasonable rent.

Bill: What's the number?

Steve: Oh! No phone! They just give an address. 3139 Pine Grove. Hey! That's just around the corner from Linda and Kim's apartment.

Bill: And three blocks from McGuire's Pub. Sounds good already. Bring along your checkbook, just in case it's available and we can pay the first month's rent and one month deposit.

Steve: Nice to travel in the company of an optimist. Look, if it's available and we take it, I'll buy the first round at McGuire's. If it's not available, you can buy the first round—to drown our sorrows and hard luck in ale.

Bill: Either way we can't lose.

Steve: Really!

[Two hours later at McGuire's Pub.]

Bill: Cheers!

Steve: Here's to the new apartment!

Bill: Man, we were really lucky to get over there so early. Did you see all those people who came in after we'd already signed the lease and given the landlord our checks?

Steve: What's our new phone number? I'd better write it down or I'll forget it.

Bill: 987-6181. Tomorrow I'll call the phone company and have it put in my name. You can call the gas company and ask them to connect the gas.

Steve: Tomorrow's Sunday and Monday is Labor Day. Is Tuesday okay with you?

Bill: Right! I forgot. Isn't that terrific that the electricity is included in the rent? That's a lucky break!

Steve: And unusual too. And the stove and refrigerator come included even though it's listed as an unfurnished apartment.

Bill: I think all apartments come with a stove, refrigerator, and sink. I've never heard of any that didn't. Let's call Dick and see if he's using his VW bus tomorrow. If not, we can borrow it to move our stuff in right away.

Steve: I think I'll pack my sound system in boxes tonight. I'd hate for any traveling to damage it. It's really delicate equipment.

Bill: Good idea! Plus, we'll want music for the party.

Steve: Party?

Bill: Sure! We'll have to inaugurate the place Monday after we're moved in. Right?

Steve: Right!

COMPREHENSION QUESTIONS

1. How old do you think Bill and Steve are?
2. Why did Bill want to move into the new apartment before Tuesday?
3. Where is Bill's family spending the weekend? Why?
4. What are Steve's plans for next year?
5. What is McGuire's?
6. How did Bill and Steve find their new apartment?
7. Describe the apartment Bill and Steve finally rented.
8. How did Bill find out about Steve's promotion? Why didn't Steve tell him in the first place?

9. What major debts does Steve have that he wants to pay off as soon as possible?

10. Where do Kim and Linda live? Who are they?

VOCABULARY

Words Used in Dialog

ad
available
basement
beanbag chair
checkbook
cheers*
cozy
deposit
down payment
fireplace
firewood
furnished
high-rise
inaugurate
Labor Day*
landlord
lease
limit
limitation
newspaper stand
parquet
penthouse
salary
sensitive
sink
stove
sun deck
unfurnished
want ads
waterbed

Phrases

around the corner
first round*
Here's to . . .*
immediate occupancy
in comfort
in the long run*
just in case
lucky break*
sound system*
top rent figure

Verbs

buy out
catch the eye*
contact
damage
drown (our) sorrow*
go higher*
include
keep it under*
leave speechless
look promising
move in
post
put it in (my) name*
store (away)*
take (an apartment)*
take a look

Slang

get off my back*
Really!
stuff
take off (on a trip)*

VOCABULARY REVIEW

around the corner
catches my eye
drowned their sorrow
first round
go any higher
just in case
left me speechless
lucky break
be posted
(to) store

A. Rewrite the following sentences, replacing the italicized portion with a word or phrase in the Vocabulary Review above.

1. The two friends *forgot about their problems* by drinking beer until four o'clock in the morning.
2. His political statement *left me without anything to say.*
3. Every summer I *put* all my ski equipment in the attic of my parents' home.
4. I like this apartment, but three hundred dollars is all I can afford; I don't think I can *pay any more than that.*
5. I probably won't find anything I need, but just in case, I'll go to the bazaar and see if anything *attracts my attention.*

B. Use the following phrases in original sentences:

1. first round
2. catches my eye
3. looks promising
4. in the long run
5. off my back

C. Put an L after each of the words which you feel pertains to a luxury penthouse apartment; put a B after each word you feel is associated with an inexpensive budget apartment. Some words may fall into both categories.

balcony
basement
beanbag chair
cozy
fireplace
high-rise
kitchenette
linoleum
parquet
reasonable
refrigerator
stove
sun deck
waterbed

QUESTIONS FOR DISCUSSION

1. Is it customary in your country for young people like Bill and Steve to live away from home before they are married? Do you think this is a good idea? Explain your answer.
2. How are apartments rented in your native country? How does that compare with the scene you just read?
3. What are some long-term goals and short-term goals of each of the two young men? Are these goals drastically different from the goals of young men in your native country?
4. In the story it appeared very easy for the two young men to find and rent an apartment. Would it have been just as easy if Bill and Steve had been two foreign exchange students in the United States? What differences might there have been? What problems can you foresee?
5. How do you think the parents of Bill and Steve will react to their sons moving out into an apartment? Would parents in your native country react any differently? If so, how? Would there be any difference if they were young women instead of young men? How?
6. What are some advantages and disadvantages of renting a furnished apartment? An unfurnished apartment? If you rent an apartment, which kind do you rent? Why?

SUGGESTED ACTIVITIES

1. Discuss and then write a composition in which you describe the differences in the living style of the young people in the United States and the young people in your native country.
2. Have you ever tried to rent your own apartment? Share your experiences with other students.
3. With several other members of the class prepare a mini-drama in which you depict a problem situation in apartment hunting. For example, a young couple, wife pregnant, with two small children, two dogs, one cat, and a bird, talking to a prospective landlord.
4. Bring in want ads from a United States newspaper advertising apartments. "Translate" the abbreviated language in the ads into understandable English.

STANDARD APARTMENT LEASE

This Indenture, MADE the day of

in the year of our Lord one thousand nine hundred and

Witnesseth, That

do hereby lease, demise, and let unto

To hold for the term of

from the day of nineteen hundred and

yielding and paying therefor the rent of

And said Lessee do promise to pay the said rent in

and to quit and deliver up the premises to the Lessor , attorney, peaceably and quietly, at the end of the term, in as good order and condition, reasonable use and wearing thereof, fire and other unavoidable casualties excepted, as the same now are, or may be put in to by the said Lessor , and to pay the rent as above stated, during the term, and also the rent as above stated, for such further time as the Lessee may hold the same, and not make or suffer any waste thereof; nor lease, nor underlet, nor permit any other person or persons to occupy or improve the same, or make or suffer to be made any alteration therein, but with the approbation of the Lessor thereto, in writing, having been first obtained; and that the Lessor may enter to view and make improvements, and to expel the Lessee , if he shall fail to pay the rent as aforesaid, or make or suffer any strip or waste thereof.

And provided also, that in case the premises, or any part thereof during said term, be destroyed or damaged by fire or other unavoidable casualty, so that the same shall be thereby rendered unfit for use and habitation, then and in such case, the rent hereinbefore reserved, or a just and proportional part thereof, according to the nature and extent of the injuries sustained, shall be suspended or abated until the said premises shall have been put in proper condition for use and habitation by the said Lessor , or these presents shall thereby be determined and ended at the election of the said Lessor or legal representatives.

In witness whereof, The said parties have hereunto interchangeably set their hands and seals the day and year first above written.

Signed and sealed in presence of

.... } ....

.... } ....

5. Explore ways of finding apartments other than through the want ads: university housing service, special bulletin boards, agencies, special publications. Report your findings to the class.
6. Bring to class pictures from magazines which show the kind of kitchen, dining room, living room, bedroom, etc., that you'd like to have in your "dream apartment." Describe them to the class.
7. Investigate the proper procedure to be followed in your community or town for connecting a new phone, or electricity, etc., for a new apartment or house. Report the correct process to the class.

GLOSSARY

Vocabulary

Cheers!—a toast, said before drinking.
Labor Day—the United States workingman's holiday, celebrated on the first Monday of September.

Phrases

first round—the first group of drinks.
Here's to . . .—the beginning of a toast to someone or something.
in the long run—eventually.
lucky break—fortunate opportunity.
sound system—record-playing components, for example, a turntable and loudspeakers.

Verbs

catch the eye—attract attention.
drown (our) sorrow—drink to forget some unhappiness.
go higher—pay more.
keep it under—pay less than.
put it in (my) name—sign for ownership or responsibility.
store away—pack or put in storage.
take (an apartment)—rent.

Nonstandard English

get off my back—don't bother me.
take off (on a trip)—leave.

CAPSULE TEN

Family Clean-Up

DIALOG

Ms. Scott: Mary, John, Adam. Time to get up. Breakfast will be ready in ten minutes.

[Silence.]

Ms. Scott: Rise and shine. Everybody up for breakfast in ten minutes.

Mr. Scott: Do you really expect any response at 8:05 on a Saturday morning? My, but you are an optimist!

Ms. Scott: Perhaps, but if we're going to go to the lake next weekend with the Swansons, everyone has to pitch in today to get the yard ready for summer.

Mr. Scott: Well, I do seem to recall such a discussion at the dinner table one evening.

Ms. Scott: Everyone enjoys the yard all summer, so I think everyone should help put it in shape.

Mr. Scott: Okay. I'm with you all the way.

[He walks to the stairs and calls.]

Breakfast will be on the table in three minutes. The last person to be seated will wash the breakfast dishes.

[There is a loud noise and the thunder of feet is heard as the three Scott children race downstairs to the breakfast table.]

Adam: I'm first, Dad. I got here first. No dishes for me.

Mary: You got here first because you pushed like an elephant down the stairs. Anyway, I'm second.

John: You are not second. You got to the table second, but I sat down before you did.

Mary: Daddy said, "To the table," he didn't say, "To sit down."

John: He said, "To be seated." Didn't you, Dad?

Ms. Scott: Children, please. Eat your breakfast. I'll do the dishes. I think there's enough work to go around.

Adam: Wow! Pancakes and bacon. Great, Mom! But what's so special? It isn't Sunday. This is what we usually have on Sunday.

Ms. Scott: Since everyone will be working so hard today, I thought you'd need some extra energy and a good send-off.

Mary: Send-off? Where are we going? And what's all this talk about work? I have a tennis date at 11:00 with Liz Caster.

John: Yes! And I was going to help Peter Cass fix up his motorcycle.

Ms. Scott: What's this about tennis and motorcycles? I thought we all agreed to work together today so that next weekend, Memorial Day, we could go with the Swansons to their summer cottage, at the lake.

John: Oh! I forgot all about it.

Mary: Me too! Gee, Mom, I really need to practice tennis for my P.E. class.

John: I sure hate to let down an old friend like Peter. He's counting on me to help him.

Mr. Scott: Well, who are you going to let down? An old friend like Peter or your own family?

John: Yes, Dad. I guess you've got a point.

Adam: Great pancakes, Mom. Any more maple syrup?

Ms. Scott: Thank you, Adam. Yes, here's another bottle.

Mary: Well, I guess I can postpone my tennis game to tomorrow afternoon. What do you want me to do, Mom?

Ms. Scott: I thought you could take the patio furniture out of the garage and put it in the yard and wash it down with the hose. At the same time you could hose off the screens before your father hangs them.

Mr. Scott: I'm going to take down all the storm windows and hang up the screens. John, after you get the screens down from the attic in the garage, you could put the storm windows up there for summer storage.

John: Okay, Dad. Anything else?

Mr. Scott: Could you also put up the back screen door?

Adam: I'll paint the doghouse.

Ms. Scott: Good idea, Adam. It sat outside in the rain and snow all winter and it looks horrible.

John: Adam gets all the breaks!

Mr. Scott: Well, Son. Since you enjoy painting so much, you can also give a fresh coat of paint to the back fence.

Adam: But, Dad. That's a big job!

John: A big job for a big man!

Mr. Scott: I'm sure you can do it well, Son.

Adam: I'm going to take my transistor radio with me to listen to the ball game while I'm painting, okay?

Mr. Scott: Just so you get the job done, and done well. When you're finished would you please mow the lawn?

Adam: But I just cut the grass a few days ago.

Ms. Scott: A few days ago! I believe it was more like two weeks ago. Anyway, it needs to be mowed again. Mary, after you've washed the patio furniture, you can help me pull weeds in the garden.

Mary: Oh, Mom! That just ruins my hands and fingernails. Do I have to?

Ms. Scott: Young lady, I believe you enjoy fresh vegetables as much as the rest of the family. And a garden doesn't grow by itself. It must be weeded. I have an extra pair of rubber gloves you can wear.

Mr. Scott: Let's get this show on the road. Sounds like everybody's got something to do.

Adam: Hey! Can we cook out for lunch, Mom? Can we have barbecued hamburgers cooked outside?

Mary: We've just finished breakfast and already you're asking about lunch. Is food all you ever think about?

Ms. Scott: I had planned to run over to McDonald's and bring back hamburgers for lunch. But if one of you will go down to the basement and bring up the grill and wash it off, I think we can cook outside for supper tonight.

Adam: Oh, I'll bring it up, Mom. Right now, I have to go to the basement anyway to get the paint for the doghouse. Wow! Hamburgers cooked outside for dinner tonight. I can't wait.

COMPREHENSION QUESTIONS

1. Why is the Scott family cleaning up the yard this weekend?
2. Who will wash the breakfast dishes?
3. What does the Scott family usually have for breakfast on Sunday morning?
4. Who do you think is the youngest of the three children? Why?

5. What will the Scott family do on Memorial Day weekend?
6. Where will the Scott family have dinner tonight?
7. Where has the doghouse been all winter?
8. Who are the Swansons? What relation are they to the Scotts?
9. How did Mr. Scott get the children to come quickly to the breakfast table?
10. Where was the grill kept all winter?

VOCABULARY

Words Used in Dialog

attic	lawn	screens
basement	Memorial Day	storm windows
decision	optimist	summer cottage
fence	pancakes	weeded
hose	P.E. class	yard
invitation	response	

Phrases

enough to go around*	in shape	with you all the way*
get the job done*	Rise and shine	work laid out
get this show on the road*	send-off	you've got a point*

Verbs

accept	have his share	postpone
cook out	hose off	pull weeds
count on*	hurry up	recall
cut (the grass)	let down*	wash down*
do (the dishes)	mow	wash up (dishes)
fix up	pitch in*	

VOCABULARY REVIEW

accept	count on	gets the breaks
ago	do (dishes)	get this show on the road
anyway	get in shape	to go around

hurry up
optimist
pitch in
postpone
pull weeds
recall
ruin
send-off
you've got a point
work laid out

A. Replace the italicized portion with the appropriate word or phrase listed in the Vocabulary Review above to form a meaningful sentence.

1. My brother never does anything today he can *put off* until tomorrow.
2. Would you help me *wash* the dishes?
3. John is a *person who always sees the bright side of any situation.*
4. The football players need to *build their bodies up* again after the long holiday vacation.
5. You have enough *work to do* to keep you busy for three weeks!
6. You can always *rely on* Adam for help.
7. He can't *remember* where he left his books.
8. I don't agree with you completely, but *you are right* on that one issue.
9. If we all *help out,* this work will be done in a very short time.
10. There's enough food *for everybody.*

B. Use each group of words and phrases in the given order, and form them to make an original and meaningful sentence.

Example: Sue / play tennis / do dishes / anyway
Sue wants to play tennis but she must do the dishes anyway.

1. weather / ruin / holiday weekend
2. sister / do (dishes) / every night
3. family / cook out / nice weather
4. everyone / pitch in / summer cottage / in shape
5. hamburgers / to go around

C. Write original sentences using the following phrases:

1. let down
2. gets the breaks
3. get this show on the road
4. with you all the way
5. get in shape

QUESTIONS FOR DISCUSSION

1. On the basis of information in the dialog, what do you think the Scott family income is? Explain. How do you think this compares with most other American families?
2. How can we tell that this scene took place in a town? What differences would there be in this scene if it took place in the country, as opposed to a town or city?
3. The United States has been called the "Do-It-Yourself" nation. What does this mean? Do you think it is true? Is this true in your native country as well? If not, why not?
4. What kind of relationship do you think the Scott children have with their parents? Is the relationship between the Scott children and their parents any different from the typical child-parent relationship in your native country? If so, how?
5. What impact do you think television, the telephone, and rapid transportation have had on family unity?
6. Do you think family unity is important to society? Why or why not? How do you think family unity is accomplished?

SUGGESTED ACTIVITIES

1. Memorial Day is celebrated May 30 in the United States to honor the memory of those who lost their lives in service to their country. The day has also become one for personal remembrance: for visiting and decorating the graves of family and friends, and for honoring their memories. It was first known as Decoration Day. If

your native country has a similar holiday, make a short oral report to the class explaining why, when, and how the day is celebrated.

2. Discuss with the class and then write a composition about typical weekend activities in your native country.

4. With several other members of the class construct a mini-drama in which a teenage son has asked his father's permission to use the family car for the evening, and the father has just given his permission when the mother walks in and overhears. She says the son should not be given permission because he did not clean his room as she had asked him to do when he came home from school.

3. Describe in oral and/or written form a typical Saturday or Sunday breakfast in your native country.

GLOSSARY

Phrases

enough to go around—enough for everyone.
get the breaks—have good luck.
get the job done—finish the work.
get this show on the road—get moving; start acting instead of talking.
with you all the way—support for someone or his ideas.
you've got a point—your idea has merit or reason.

Verbs

count on—depend on.
let (someone) down—not fulfill your part of an agreement.
pitch in—help with the work.
wash down—clean something well with soap and water.

VOCABULARY REVIEW, CAPSULES 7 to 10

to accept
to account for
anyway
a total loss
checkbook
comes in handy
to count on
to damage
down payment
easy-payment plan
to fix (something) up
to furnish
get in shape
gets all the breaks
go any higher
going in circles
going on
just in case
laid off
lease
looks promising
to move in
to mow
parquet
to pitch in
to put (someone) out of (home)
to recall
sensitive
unfurnished
vinyl
want ads
to wash down
you've got a point

Which of the words or phrases listed above could be used meaningfully in the following sentences? It may be necessary to make changes in the forms of the words.

1. Many people are tricked into believing that they purchased real leather, when in reality they bought a synthetic material called ____________.

2. If something no longer has any value, it might be called ____________.

3. People who go around and around discussing the same problem without ever reaching any decision are often ____________.

4. Companies offer an ____________ which often includes a low down-payment, monthly installment payments, and high interest rates.

5. If you have to explain the reason behind something that you have done, then you must ____________ your actions.

6. If it is five minutes before one o'clock, you might hear someone say that it's ____________ one o'clock.

7. The best place to look for an apartment is in the ______________ of the Sunday paper.

8. If he comes home late once more, his parents have threatened ______________.

9. A person who has been let go from his job has been ______________.

10. I don't think it's essential to have an electric drill, but it sure ______________ when you need to fix something around the house.

11. The landlord of this apartment insisted that we sign a two-year ______________.

12. In order to buy that house you will need a ______________ of 20 percent of the total price.

13. Be sure to take your umbrella ______________ it starts to rain.

14. My new job isn't certain yet, but the lady who interviewed me said that it ______________.

15. I can pay $280 for rent, but I can't ______________.

16. Joe is really a lucky guy. He sure ______________.

17. They bought an old house that needs a lot of work; little by little they plan to ______________.

18. After sitting at home all winter, I feel I must try to swim at least three times a week in order to ______________.

19. Whenever there's a problem to be solved, you ______________ Eva to help out.

20. If this job is going to be finished today, then everyone must ______________.

PRETEST

This test may be given to students prior to their working with the culture capsules in order to determine if they need to study all the capsules. There are four questions relating to each capsule. If a student answers correctly all four questions of one specific capsule, the teacher may want to eliminate that particular capsule for that student. In this way the material may be individualized to different students within a large class. The pretest may also be given before working with the capsules as a means of measuring how much students have learned, by comparing the results of the pretest with those of the posttest, which should be given upon completion of all the capsules.

1. Rush hour means
   (a) heavy traffic (b) rushing around (c) college registration
2. Crossing the street in the middle of the block is
   (a) legal (b) jaywalking (c) safer than crossing at the corner
3. One ethnic group replacing another in a specific area of a city is an example of
   (a) inner-urban development (b) a changing neighborhood (c) religious prejudice
4. In many large cities trucks are permitted to drive only in the two right-hand lanes of
   (a) all streets (b) boulevards (c) expressways
5. Towels and linens often go on sale in the United States every
   (a) August (b) July 4th (c) Christmas
6. The school year in the United States is usually from
   (a) September to June (b) March to October (c) August to March
7. Divorced women in the United States are generally
   (a) not respected (b) considered strange (c) accepted socially
8. Alimony is money
   (a) paid by the ex-husband to his ex-wife for the children's expenses (b) put in the bank for the children's education (c) paid by the ex-husband to his ex-wife for her support

9. A charge account permits you to
(a) shop without cash (b) borrow money (c) buy only with cash

10. A gift certificate permits you to
(a) pay later (b) pick out your own gift (c) certify the gift

11. You must know your neck size and arm length in order to buy
(a) turtleneck sweaters (b) jackets (c) shirts

12. To bump into someone is
(a) to meet accidentally (b) to have a fight (c) to be bothered

13. Fresh fruits and vegetables are
(a) preserved foods (b) produce (c) groceries

14. Nutrition is the study of
(a) nuts (b) good eating (c) cooking

15. Granola is a
(a) popular ten-speed bicycle (b) natural cereal (c) health-food restaurant

16. A vegetarian eats
(a) only vegetables (b) no meat (c) only nuts and dried fruits

17. Bloomingdale's and Macy's are famous New York
(a) department stores (b) restaurants (c) art galleries

18. An M.A. degree is taken
(a) before a B.A. (b) after the Ph.D. (c) after the B.A.

19. Among other things, a receptionist must
(a) answer the telephone (b) clean the office (c) serve lunch

20. People bid against each other to buy items at
(a) an auction (b) a yard sale (c) a bazaar

21. A "junk-food freak" would like to eat
(a) granola (b) Cocoa-Cola and popcorn (c) steak and mashed potatoes

22. Contacts are
(a) glass sculptures (b) contracts with a doctor (c) a form of eyeglasses

23. Which of the following is not a childhood disease?
(a) appendicitis (b) chicken pox (c) measles

24. To purchase certain medication in the United States you need a doctor's
(a) receipt (b) perception (c) prescription

25. Dixie is
(a) a popular southern drink (b) one way of referring to the South (c) a famous dress designer

26. A car with loading space in the back instead of a trunk is called a
(a) convertible (b) station wagon (c) hard top

27. A car note refers to
(a) a loan for a car (b) the title of the car (c) ownership papers

28. In slang English, if you don't have any "bread," you don't have any
(a) food (b) money (c) a house

29. Someone who faces his responsibilities
(a) accepts them (b) denies them (c) gives them to someone else

30. If you've been laid off the job, you have been
(a) transferred (b) promoted (c) fired

31. Someone agrees with you if he says you
(a) are in the same boat (b) hit the nail on the head (c) are coming right up

32. A plant is
(a) a factory (b) a yard (c) a farm

33. In order to rent an apartment, you often are required to sign a
(a) landlord (b) lease (c) loan

34. If you want someone to stop bothering you, you might tell him to
(a) drown his sorrows (b) get off your back (c) keep it under his hat

35. If something catches your eye, you
(a) are attracted to it (b) are repulsed by it (c) can't see it

36. If something looks promising, it
(a) has possibilities (b) is a solemn oath (c) bothers you

37. To put off doing something is
(a) to start doing it (b) to continue doing it (c) to postpone doing it

38. If you can count on a person, you can
(a) rely on him (b) recall him (c) correct him

39. If someone lets you down, he
(a) counted on you (b) disappointed you (c) let you fall down

40. Someone who gets all the breaks
(a) is unlucky (b) has accidents (c) is lucky

POSTTEST

This posttest may be given to students after they have completed their work with the culture capsules. The results of this test should be compared with the results of the pretest in the event that the teacher wants to measure cultural learning before and after the work with the capsules.

1. Which of the following does not refer to heavy traffic?
(a) rush hour (b) traffic jam (c) merging traffic

2. Jaywalking is
(a) walking across an expressway (b) crossing the street "against the light" (c) crossing the street in the middle of the block

3. A "changing neighborhood" refers to
(a) a commercial area (b) one ethnic group replacing another (c) urban renewal

4. Trucks are not allowed to drive on
(a) boulevards (b) expressways (c) Sundays

5. At an August White Sale you can buy
(a) summer bathing suits (b) sails for a boat (c) sheets and towels

6. The "Back-to-School" season in the United States generally is in
(a) September (b) January (c) June

7. In the United States there is little social stigma attached to
(a) divorced men (b) divorced women (c) divorced men *and* women

8. Money paid from the ex-husband to help support the ex-wife is called
(a) child support (b) alimony (c) a trust fund

9. You can shop without money if you have a
(a) savings account (b) charge account (c) checking account

10. A polite way to give a gift of money is in the form of a
(a) charge account (b) gift certificate (c) certified check

11. If you asked for a size 15½/32, you would be buying
(a) pants (b) a shirt (c) a jacket

12. To accidentally meet someone unexpectedly is to
(a) run after someone (b) run into someone (c) run over someone

13. Which of the following is an example of produce?
(a) lettuce (b) peanut butter (c) homemade jelly

14. People interested in healthful eating habits are concerned about
(a) gourmet cooking (b) nutrition (c) dieting

15. A natural cereal made without preservatives is
(a) corn flakes (b) granola (c) yogurt

16. If you wanted to read something about healthful eating habits, you might read a book by
(a) Adele Davis (b) Julia Child (c) James Beard

17. Two famous stores in New York, considered to be of a high quality, are
(a) Sears and Roebuck (b) Bloomingdale's and Lord & Taylor (c) E.J. Korvette and K Mart

18. You study for a master's degree
(a) after the doctoral degree (b) after the bachelor's degree (c) before the bachelor's degree

19. A receptionist has

(a) more responsibility than a secretary (b) the same responsibilities as a secretary (c) less responsibility than a secretary

20. If you are moving from a house and want to sell things you no longer need at a cheap price, you might consider having

(a) an auction (b) a yard sale (c) a budget basement

21. A "junk-food freak" would be least likely to select

(a) yogurt (b) ice cream (c) frozen custard

22. Which of the following is a form of eyeglasses?

(a) contacts (b) sun visor (c) goggles

23. Which of the following is not a childhood disease?

(a) whooping cough (b) mumps (c) appendicitis

24. When the doctor writes down the name of the medicine which you will then purchase at the pharmacy, it is called a

(a) perception (b) prescription (c) receipt

25. Which of the following expressions refers to the South?

(a) Dixie (b) the sun belt (c) sunset strip

26. Which of the following model of cars provides the most ventilation?

(a) sun roof (b) station wagon (c) convertible

27. Monthly installments paid for a car are provided by

(a) car note (b) a mortgage (c) credit card payments

28. In English slang, if you don't have any "bread"

(a) you're out of dough (b) you're in the pink (c) you have lots of money

29. If you accept something, you

(a) postpone it (b) face it (c) accomplish it

30. To be fired means to be

(a) burned (b) laid off (c) excited

31. If someone tells you that you hit the nail on the head, you know that

(a) you are right (b) you didn't understand it (c) you both feel the same way

32. A factory is the same as a
(a) plant (b) warehouse (c) stockyard

33. The person who owns an apartment house is the
(a) superintendent (b) landlord (c) tenant

34. If you want to drown your sorrows, you want
(a) to forget your problems (b) someone to quit bothering you (c) to keep it under your hat

35. You are attracted by something if it
(a) catches your eye (b) gets off your back (c) gets all the breaks

36. Something which has possibilities
(a) is laid off (b) is postponed (c) looks promising

37. To procrastinate means
(a) to put off (b) to put on (c) to put up with

38. Someone you can count on is
(a) dependable (b) unreliable (c) an accountant

39. If you counted on someone and he let you down,
(a) he relied on you (b) he disappointed you (c) he lived up to expectations

40. A lucky person
(a) gets all the breaks (b) is broke (c) is broken up

ANSWER KEY TO VOCABULARY REVIEWS

Vocabulary Review, Capsules 1 to 3

1. commuting
2. jaywalking
3. expressway
4. high-rise apartments
5. rush-hour traffic
6. shopping centers
7. August White Sale
8. making ends meet
9. babysitter
10. out of touch
11. gift certificate
12. to charge it
13. range
14. conservative
15. bumped into

Vocabulary Review, Capsules 4 to 6

1. vegetarian
2. novelty has worn off
3. stock up on
4. take (them) up on it
5. in a pinch
6. wasting his life away
7. complicated
8. to live off
9. coming right up
10. to take the edge off
11. junk-food freak
12. as fit as a fiddle
13. run down
14. prescription
15. to take off

Vocabulary Review, Capsules 7 to 10

1. vinyl
2. a total loss
3. going in circles
4. easy-payment plan
5. account for
6. going on
7. want ads
8. to put him out of the house
9. laid off
10. comes in handy
11. lease
12. down payment
13. just in case
14. looks promising
15. go any higher
16. gets all the breaks
17. fix it up
18. get in shape
19. can count on
20. pitch in

ANSWER KEY TO PRETEST

1. a – heavy traffic
2. b – jaywalking
3. b – changing neighborhood
4. c – expressways
5. a – August
6. a – September to June
7. c – accepted socially
8. c – paid by the ex-husband to his ex-wife for her support
9. a – shop without cash
10. b – pick out your own gift
11. c – shirts
12. a – to meet accidentally
13. b – produce
14. b – good eating
15. b – natural cereal
16. b – no meat
17. a – department stores
18. c – after the B.A.
19. a – answer the telephone
20. a – an auction
21. b – Coca-Cola and popcorn
22. c – a form of eyeglasses
23. a – appendicitis
24. c – prescription
25. b – one way of referring to the South
26. b – station wagon
27. a – a loan for a car
28. b – money
29. a – accepts them
30. c – fired
31. b – hit the nail on the head
32. a – a factory
33. b – lease
34. b – get off your back
35. a – are attracted to it
36. a – has possibilities
37. c – to postpone doing it
38. a – rely on him
39. b – disappointed you
40. c – is lucky

ANSWER KEY TO POSTTEST

1. c – merging traffic
2. c – crossing the street in the middle of the block
3. b – one ethnic group replacing another
4. a – boulevards
5. c – sheets and towels
6. a – September
7. c – divorced men and women
8. b – alimony
9. b – charge account
10. b – gift certificate
11. b – a shirt
12. b – run into someone
13. a – lettuce
14. b – nutrition
15. b – granola
16. a – Adele Davis
17. b – Bloomingdale's and Lord & Taylor
18. b – after the bachelor's degree
19. c – less responsibility than a secretary
20. b – a yard sale
21. a – yogurt
22. a – contacts
23. c – appendicitis
24. b – prescription
25. a – Dixie
26. c – convertible
27. a – a car note
28. a – you're out of dough
29. b – face it
30. b – laid off
31. c – you both feel the same way
32. a – plant
33. b – landlord
34. a – to forget your problems
35. a – catches your eye
36. c – looks promising
37. a – to put off
38. a – dependable
39. b – he disappointed you
40. a – gets all the breaks